Lewis&Clark

From the Rockies to the Pacific

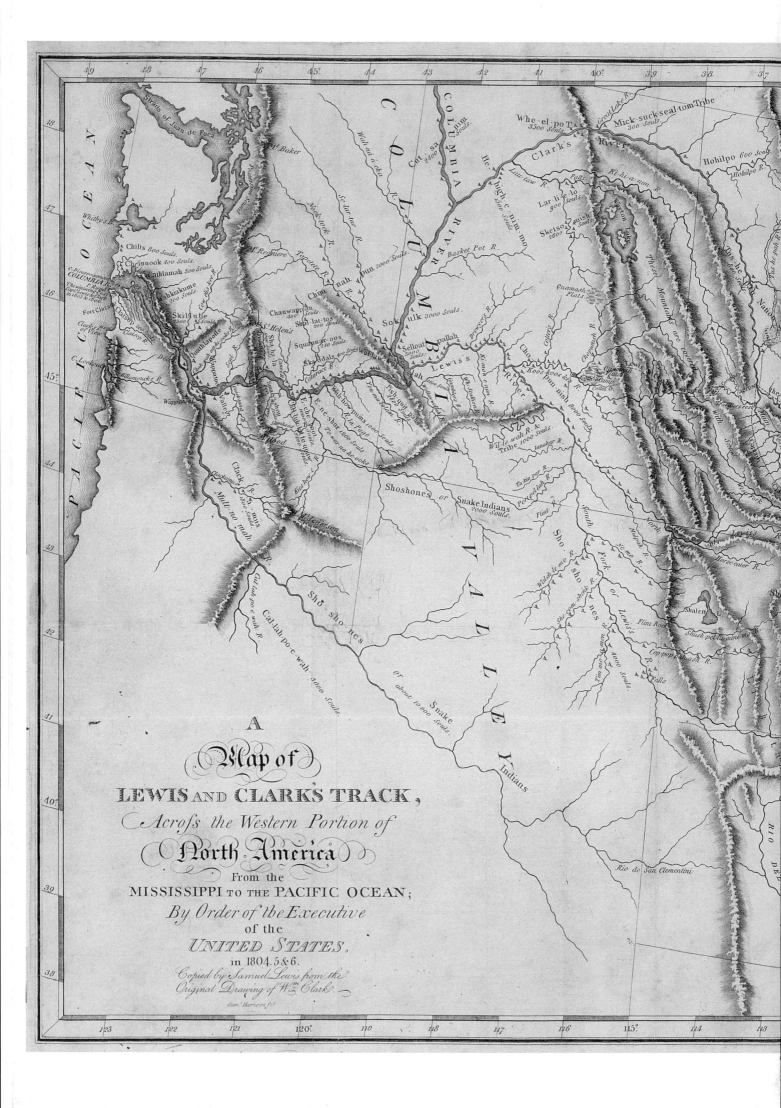

A
Map of
LEWIS AND CLARK'S TRACK,
Across the Western Portion of
North America
From the
MISSISSIPPI TO THE PACIFIC OCEAN;
By Order of the Executive
of the
UNITED STATES,
in 1804. 5 & 6.
Copied by Samuel Lewis from the
Original Drawing of Wm Clark.

Saml Harrison fc:

Lewis&Clark

From the Rockies to the Pacific

Text STEPHEN DOW BECKHAM

Photography ROBERT M. REYNOLDS

GRAPHIC ARTS CENTER PUBLISHING®

Photographs © MMII by Robert Reynolds
Text © MMII by Stephen Beckham
Book compilation © MMII by Graphic Arts Center Publishing®
An imprint of Graphic Arts Center Publishing Company
P.O. Box 10306, Portland, Oregon 97296-0306
503/226-2402
www.gacpc.com

Library of Congress Cataloging-in-Publication Data
Beckham, Stephen Dow.
    Lewis and Clark from the Rockies to the Pacific /
    by Stephen Dow Beckham ; photography by Robert M. Reynolds.
        p. cm.
Includes bibliographical references and index.
    ISBN 1-55868-645-2 (hardbound)
    1. Lewis and Clark Expedition (1804-1806) 2. Northwest,
Pacific—Discovery and exploration. 3. Oregon—Discovery and
exploration. 4. Northwest, Pacific—Description and travel.
5. Oregon—Description and travel. 6. Northwest, Pacific—Pictorial works.
7. Oregon—Pictorial works. I. Reynolds, Robert M. (Robert Moland)
II. Title.
    F592.7 .B44 2002
    917.804'2—dc21

                                                            2001007053

President: Charles M. Hopkins
Associate Publisher: Douglas A. Pfeiffer
Editorial Staff: Timothy W. Frew, Ellen Harkins Wheat,
    Tricia Brown, Jean Andrews, Kathy Matthews,
    Jean Bond-Slaughter
Production Staff: Richard L. Owsiany, Heather Doornink
Design: Robert Reynolds and Letha Wulf,
    Reynolds Wulf Inc.
Digital prepress: Color Technology, Inc.
Printer: Haagen Printing
Bindery: Lincoln & Allen Company

Printed in the United States of America

The historical photographs on pages 3 (ORHI21650#1100-A), 52 (ORHI5944#373-A), and 57
(ORHI67534#565) have been used courtesy of the Oregon Historical Society. Other historical
photographs have been used by permission of the collectors credited in the photo captions.

The photograph on page 105 has been digitally altered.

*Gate, side one: William Clark's "A Map of Lewis and Clark's Track, Across the Western Portion
of North America," drawn by Samuel Lewis from the original by William Clark, and engraved by
Samuel Harrison, 1814 (Beinecke Library at Yale University)*

Gate, left: Bitterroot Mountains east of Saddle Camp, Idaho Engelmann spruce, (Picea engelmannii)

Gate, center: Columbia River near Skamokawa, Washington

*Right: Passage of The Dalles, Columbia River, 1884 (Carlton E. Watkins, Oregon Historical Society,
Portland, Oregon)*

HISTORY

OF

THE EXPEDITION

UNDER THE COMMAND OF

CAPTAINS LEWIS AND CLARK,

TO

THE SOURCES OF THE MISSOURI.

THENCE

ACROSS THE ROCKY MOUNTAINS

AND DOWN THE

RIVER COLUMBIA TO THE PACIFIC OCEAN.

PERFORMED DURING THE YEARS 1804—5—6.

By order of the

GOVERNMENT OF THE UNITED STATES

PREPARED FOR THE PRESS

BY PAUL ALLEN, ESQUIRE.

IN TWO VOLUMES.

VOL. II.

PHILADELPHIA:
PUBLISHED BY BRADFORD AND INSKEEP; AND
E. J. COALE, BALTIMORE; A
CHARLESTON, S. C.
J. Maxwell, Printer.
1814.

Prologue

"An intelligent officer with ten or twelve chosen men, fit for the enterprize and willing to undertake it, taken from our posts, where they may be spared without inconvenience, might explore the whole line, even to the Western ocean, have conferences with the natives on the subject of commercial intercourse, get admission among them for our traders as others are admitted, agree on convenient deposits for an interchange of articles, and return with information acquired in the course of two summers."

Thomas Jefferson, Message to Congress, January 18, 1803

In September 1805, the Lewis and Clark Expedition reached the Continental Divide and the limits of the United States. When the Corps of Discovery proceeded on to the west and entered the watershed of the great Columbia River, it unleashed forces that helped transform the seventeen states then making up the United States into a continental nation reaching from sea to sea. The labors of this party met the demands of a young nation about to embark on a century of financing exploration and collecting useful information. The adventures of Lewis and Clark captured worldwide attention and spawned a flood of publications that competed to meet the resulting interest.

The following narrative examines the trek of the Lewis and Clark Expedition from the headwaters of the Missouri to the Pacific, and back to the eastern flank of the Rocky Mountains. It is an account of the travels and tribulations of a small party of explorers in one of the largest and least-known parts of North America. Maps of the American West in 1803 identified only the margins of the Pacific Coast and the lower tributaries of streams running into the Mississippi. All else was blank space and imagination. Lewis and Clark put the world into a new order. In their expedition into the unknown Pacific Northwest, they gave form and substance to the complex geography of a vast continent. Through their journals, field notes, and collections, they planted the seeds of curiosity that nurtured commerce, colonization, and conquest within the lifetimes of several in their party.

The far American West in 1800 was no virgin land. For as long as fifteen thousand years it had been home to dozens of different tribes and bands of Native Americans. They knew its moods, used its resources, named its places, and etched its face with their trails, red ochre pictographs, and hand-pecked petroglyphs. They communed with the land through spirit quests, dances, special rites of harvest, and a rich oral literature. Their tales swept from mythic times to the historic past and created a legacy of memory passed from generation to generation.

The Indian dominion of the western part of North America began to change when, in the late eighteenth century, Europeans nibbled at the edges of this region in voyages of discovery and, starting in 1769, in the colonization of California. Driven by multiple objectives—colonies, conquest, curiosity, and commerce—they began to chart the coastline and tap the region's resources. These events were inexorable forces of change.

The Lewis and Clark Expedition of 1804–6 entered a land of potentials only imagined. Between the Mandan villages of North Dakota and the estuary of the Columbia lay a vast domain unknown to the rest of the world. To the peoples of that region it was home; to others it was a place of intrigue. The travels of Lewis and Clark laid open the wonders, resources, and peoples of the high plains, Rockies, Columbia Plateau, and the Northwest Coast. This was the design of Thomas Jefferson. Three

Pages 4-5: Douglas fir, western hemlock, western red cedar —forest in the Columbia Gorge.

Above: Thomas Jefferson portrait by Charles Wilson Peale (National Park Service, Independence Park, Philadelphia, Pennsylvania)

Left: Paper cover of 1814 edition of the Lewis and Clark journals in two volumes as edited by Nicholas Biddle and Paul Allen (Lewis & Clark College, Portland, Oregon)

times in the late eighteenth century, Jefferson had tried to mount explorations to examine the interior of the continent; each time his mission had been frustrated. His election as president in 1800 and the fortuitous purchase of the Louisiana Territory in 1803 put him, at last, in the position to achieve his grand objective. Jefferson envisioned exploring not only Louisiana but all the way through to the Pacific. His plan was founded on his commitment to the Enlightenment: Jefferson was a statesman, architect, essayist, musician, gentleman farmer, slave owner, political theorist, philosopher, and ardent reader of books. A member of the American Philosophical Society, he participated in a circle of associates who had passionate interest in the world and everything in it: people, languages, minerals, geography, weather phenomena, flora, and fauna.

On June 20, 1803, Jefferson's multiple interests resounded through a letter of instruction to his young protégé, Meriwether Lewis. Jefferson laid out a mission to explore the trackless interior of the continent, from the Mandan villages on the Missouri River to the distant Pacific Ocean, and instructed Lewis to conceive of the military expedition as a great collecting enterprise. Lewis and his associate, William Clark, were to gather botanical and zoological specimens, weather data, ethnographic and linguistic notes on the tribes, geographical details to be entered onto maps complete with recordings of longitude and latitude, minerals, and information on prospects for trade. Ostensibly they were to seek the most practical route by water for commerce across North America. Jefferson envisioned the completion of the dream of Christopher Columbus—to find a route to the Indies to open the flow of goods and wealth to the nation at its terminus. Thus the president's instructions called for establishing diplomatic relations with the tribes, quelling hostilities and trying to establish networks for peace, and assessing along the route the manufactured goods most prized and useful to the Native inhabitants of the American West.

Lewis, who had served as Jefferson's private secretary and lived with him at the White House, headed off to Philadelphia to take a crash course in medicine and the making of scientific observations and collections. Members of the American Philosophical Society served as his instructors. Clark, a veteran of military service and compatriot in arms of Lewis in the 1790s, drew the assignment of recruiting and training a contingent of soldiers, voyageurs, and frontiersmen into the well-honed team required to carry out the president's instructions. Lewis next went to Pittsburgh to purchase a large keelboat and supplies, while Clark established Camp Dubois, an initial winter encampment in 1803 near the confluence of the Missouri and Mississippi Rivers.

The expedition departed in May 1804, for an arduous, upriver journey against the currents of the mighty Missouri. In late October, the captains and their crew, keelboat and pirogues laden with supplies, arrived at the Mandan villages. At the time, this was the farthest point of Euro-American penetration into the interior of the Louisiana Territory; everything to the west was terra incognita. The Corps of Discovery erected Fort Mandan and settled in for the winter on the plains of North Dakota. Lewis and Clark wrote reports, packaged specimens, engaged in ethnographic and linguistic studies, and winnowed the men to pick the team that would push through to the Pacific. In November they met Toussaint Charbonneau, who solicited employment as an interpreter. When the captains discovered that one of his young wives was a Shoshone and might assist in the purchase of horses on the flank of the distant mountains, they engaged him to join the expedition with his wife. Sacagawea, the Shoshone woman, gave birth on February 11, 1805, to Jean Baptiste Charbonneau; the infant became the youngest member of the expedition.

On April 7, 1805, the Corps of Discovery left Fort Mandan. The keelboat, loaded with specimens that included live prairie dogs and magpies, headed down the Missouri to St. Louis. The captains and the remainder of the reduced party—thirty-two men, one woman, and an infant—in six small canoes and two large pirogues set

Above: Meriwether Lewis and William Clark, portraits by Charles Wilson Peale (National Park Service, Independence Park, Philadelphia, Pennsylvania)

Right: Bitterroot (Lewisia rediviva). Collected on July 1, 1806, at Travellers' Rest, Bitterroot Valley, Montana, and named for Meriwether Lewis by Frederick Pursh in 1812.

out up the Missouri again into the unknown interior. Lewis sensed the drama of the moment and wrote: "This little fleet altho' not quite so rispectable as those of Columbus or Capt. Cook were still viewed by us with as much pleasure as those deservedly famed adventurers ever beheld theirs; and I dare say with quite as much anxiety for their safety and preservation." Lewis laid out the agenda: "we were now about to penetrate a country at least two thousand miles in width, on which the foot of civillized man had never trodden; the good or evil it had in store for us was for experiment yet to determine, and those little vessells contained every article by which we were to expect to subsist or defend ourselves."

The continuing ascent of the Missouri proved taxing, especially the month-long portage around the Great Falls in western Montana. Ahead lay more miles of river and, in the distance, mountain ranges hinting at the challenges beyond the horizon. The adventures of the Corps of Discovery in the Pacific Northwest in 1805 and 1806 were of national consequence. The expedition initiated contact with many heretofore unknown Native bands and tribes. From that moment, the fate of those peoples was irrevocably changed, for the meetings brought trade goods, knowledge of new weapons, clothing, and new diseases. The American explorers unwittingly began the undoing of thousands of years of Native lifeways.

Lewis and Clark headed a government-financed expedition. Fort Mandan and Fort Clatsop, their winter encampments on the Missouri and Columbia Rivers, were United States military posts. Although temporary, these stations buttressed American claims of "discovery" and arguments for possession. The detailed maps and observations recorded by the explorers added to the evidence succeeding generations of Americans used to craft an American empire reaching from shore to shore.

Lewis and Clark grasped the awesome potentials of the American West and wrote candidly about what they found. They described a land of astounding beauty, great distances, and rich resources. They found beaver, otter, and ermine. They described Indian fisheries that fed large Native populations. They encountered fertile soils, vast forests, and large areas of gentle climate. In its quest, the Corps of Discovery opened the Pacific Northwest to a curious world. The setting sun became the magnet drawing them, inexorably, toward the fulfillment of the dreams of Columbus and Jefferson. Ahead lay great rivers, trackless mountains, tribes, and adventures. The Lewis and Clark Expedition embarked on its rendezvous with destiny.

Left: Petroglyphs in Nez Perce country, Buffalo Eddy on the Snake River, Idaho

The Challenge of the Mountains

"The men are becoming lean and debilitated, on account of the scarcity and poor quality of the provisions on which we subsist: our horses' feet are also becoming very sore. We have, however, some hopes of getting soon out of this horrible mountainous desert, as we have discovered the appearance of a valley or level part of the country about 40 miles ahead."

Patrick Gass, September 19, 1806

The way west appeared remarkably simple. Cartographers presumed a symmetry to North America. Where the Appalachians formed the backbone between the Atlantic and the Mississippi River, the western lands surely had a comparable, single range of mountains. The "latest authorities" divined this configuration and laid it on their maps of the American West. All Lewis and Clark had to do was to take their party to the headwaters of the Missouri, cross the mountains, and descend the great "River of the West" to the Pacific Ocean. They might, perhaps, find a singular pass like the Cumberland Gap. Through that opening in the mountains—by short portage from the rivers—would flow the commerce of a young nation and that of distant Asia.

Alexander Mackenzie's map of 1801, showing his route across Canada to the Pacific in 1793, illustrated a single range of mountains running south from the Arctic Ocean. Aaron Arrowsmith's *A Map Exhibiting All the New Discoveries in the Interior Parts of North America . . . with Additions to 1802* likewise showed a powerfully persuasive single line of mountains at the headwaters of the Missouri. Arrowsmith had based the revisions to his 1795 map on the reports of Peter Fidler, a surveyor, astronomer, and fur trapper of the Hudson's Bay Company; Mackenzie's book and map; and the maritime charts of James Cook and George Vancouver.

The Corps of Discovery carried a map case filled with the latest information. Arrowsmith's enormous map was probably cut into panels, backed with linen or canvas, and folded into sections to travel with the maps of Mackenzie, David Thompson, and Vancouver, either as printed or as traced for use by the explorers. The map case's data, while accurate for the coastline and the lower Missouri, was of little use when ominous ranges of peaks appeared on all sides. The unknown West was filled with mountains, lots of mountains, and the greatest test of the journey was to find a way to traverse those ranges.

When the Corps of Discovery on July 25, 1805, reached Three Forks—the confluence of streams forming the Missouri—it was clear the maps had erred. Three rivers of nearly equal size fanned out toward majestic mountains, some with fields of snow on their slopes. The party was 2,464 miles from the mouth of the Missouri and had not yet traversed the great mountains. Clark, possessing keen geographical sense, did not hesitate. He pressed on immediately, moving his detachment up the northerly fork—the Jefferson River. He correctly ascertained that it was the most likely way to the west. The party left unexplored the Gallatin and Madison, streams taking their headwaters in the rugged Yellowstone country to the south.

The party spent the next three weeks in laborious ascent of the Jefferson River and the Beaverhead. The summer days lay hot on the land, but the men spent most of the hours fighting the swift current or wading and wrestling their dugouts, which had carried them and their baggage from the Great Falls of the Missouri, through muddy shallows. Wet and weary, they would settle in for the night, only to find plunging temperatures that caused even the heartiest to shiver beneath their allotted two blankets. The seemingly endless Missouri narrowed into swamps, islands, and channels. The water route had become an obstacle course that tested the Corps as it pressed against terrain and calendar.

"We renewed our march early, though the morning was very disagreeable, and proceeded over the most terrible mountains I ever beheld. . . . The snow fell so thick, and the day was so dark, that a person could not see to a distance of 200 yards." Patrick Gass, September 16, 1805

Left: Bitterroot Mountains west of Papoose Saddle, Idaho

Above: Compass of the period of Lewis and Clark (Douglas Erickson Collection, Portland, Oregon)

Timing was critical. Summer was at its peak, but the men had expended nearly four months in ascending the Missouri from Fort Mandan. If they did not move quickly, they would lose their chance to get through the mountains. The only prospect was to press on as rapidly as possible or come to terms with turning back. The journals are mostly mute on the realities that assuredly must have troubled the leaders. The transit of the Jefferson River slowed to a wearing, toilsome crawl. Mosquitoes, gnats, and biting flies plagued the men. Several had boils ulcerating on their bodies. For days William Clark persevered as a boil grew on his ankle and finally erupted. The affliction provoked him to refer to it as a "rageing fury of a tumer on my anckle musle." Others had stone bruises on their feet. Patrick Gass fell and injured his back, crashing down on the gunwale of one of the canoes. The injury was so painful that his only recourse was to walk on shore. Toussaint Charbonneau also nursed a sore ankle.

Beavers had dammed portions of the Jefferson. Sloughs, bayous, and ponds lay on all sides. At night the men found it necessary to cut piles of brush in order to lay out their blankets on a stable surface, so extensive was the mud in the river bottom. In other places the river was filled with shoals and riffles. The only way to advance was to pull the vessels through. When they had time at night, they hurried their meal and in the waning twilight dressed skins and sewed new moccasins.

The watershed of the Jefferson lay on the eastern face of the mountains, and the area contained game in abundance. The hunters found deer, elk, antelope, beaver, ducks, geese, cranes, and one day, a panther. Lewis penned descriptions of the animals and he and Clark continued to christen the streams that they encountered. Their choices of names confirmed that they were an extraordinary pair of leaders. On July 31 they dubbed a stream flowing from the southwest the "River Philosophy." On August 4 they named two others streams the "Philanthropy" and the "Wisdom." Never before in the exploration of the continent had a party invoked such noble elements of human interest.

Lewis grew increasingly anxious. The only way the party could get over the mountains was to secure horses. On August 1 he set out ahead. Lewis's venturing was nothing new; he seemed unable to contain his desire to get to places first. He had rushed ahead to be the first to view the Great Falls of the Missouri. Clark, without comment in his journal, acquiesced in his associate's hunger. Was it a quest for glory that drove Lewis? Or was it a sense of adventure? Perhaps both were at work.

The Corps of Discovery had entered the homeland of the Shoshones. At Three Forks, Sacagawea identified the place where, some five years before, a war party of Minetarees had attacked and carried her and others off as captives. She also identified Beaverhead Rock. Lewis wrote: "the Indian woman recognized the point of a high plain to our right which she informed us was not very distant from the summer retreat of her nation on a river beyond the mountains which runs to the west."

The strategy was to find Sacagawea's tribe, barter for horses, abandon the watercraft, and continue west by land. The only way in which the plan could succeed, however, was to locate the Shoshones and persuade them to trade. The prospect was problematic, for the Shoshones remained invisible. The land was vast; the way was unknown. Lewis wrote on August 8 that it was "now all important with us to meet with those people as soon as possible." To achieve that objective, he planned to split from the main party under Clark's command, cross the mountains to the Columbia, and go down that river until he found Indians. "In short it is my resolution to find them or some others who have horses," he wrote, "if it should cause me a trip of one month, for without horses we shall be obliged to leave a great part of our stores."

Lewis, George Drouillard, John Shields, and Hugh McNeal moved up the Beaverhead. Travel on land was relatively easy for the men on foot. They had to watch, however, for prickly pears and rattlesnakes. Lewis estimated that his patrol covered thirty miles the first day. On August 11, the men entered a ravine leading to a pass at the head of the stream. Lewis dispatched Drouillard to his right to follow the

creek and Shields to his left, while he and McNeal continued their course. The men had proceeded about five miles when Lewis saw an Indian man coming toward them on horseback. Watching through his spyglass, Lewis perceived that the man was armed with only bow and arrows and rode an "eligant" horse without a saddle. "I was overjoyed at the sight of this stranger," wrote Lewis, "and had no doubt of obtaining a friendly introduction to his nation provided I could get near enough to him to convince him of our being whitemen."

After Lewis's party had advanced about a mile, the Indian saw the men and all stopped. This was a moment of initial contact; Lewis was eager for it to go well. He unfastened his blanket, grasped it at two corners, and threw it in the air above his head three times, executing what was a signal of friendship among the Indians of the upper Missouri. "This signal of the robe has arisen from a custom among all those nations of spreading a robe or skin for their g[u]ests to set on when they are visited," he wrote. The Indian made no response, but he watched as Drouillard and Shields, unaware of his presence, continued to advance toward him. Lewis was desperate, for neither of the men seemed to notice the Indian watching them. Lewis was unable to signal them to halt. Lewis thus thrust his hands into his pack and grabbed beads and a looking glass, laid down his gun and pouch, and with McNeal advanced toward the stranger.

Tension gripped Lewis. He had to make contact, but when he got within two hundred feet, the man turned his horse and retreated. Desperate, Lewis shouted at him "*tab-ba-bone, tab-ba-bone,*" a word which he thought meant "I am a white man!" The term did not have the desired result; in spite of Lewis's ardent efforts, stripping away his shirt sleeve to reveal the pallor of his arm, the Indian wheeled his horse about, applied the whip, and—in an instant—vanished into the willow thickets. "I fe[l]t soarly chagrined at the conduct of the men particularly Shields to whom I principally attributed the failure in obtaining an introduction to the natives," wrote Lewis.

The meeting with the Shoshones was deferred. Lewis and his small contingent moved on. On August 12 the men ascended a creek that led to Lemhi Pass—the long-sought Continental Divide. Lewis wrote movingly of the event:

> At the distance of 4 miles further the road took us to the most distant fountain of the waters of the mighty Missouri in surch of which we have spent so many toilsome days and wristless nights. thus far I had accomplished one of those great objects on which my mind has been unalterably fixed for many years, judge then the pleasure I felt in allying my thirst with this pure ice cold water which issues from the base of a low mountain or hill of gentle ascent for ½ a mile.

The moment of fulfillment was not exclusively that of Lewis. McNeal, some two miles down the ravine, stood astride the rivulet and, as Lewis noted, "thanked his god that he had lived to bestride the mighty heretofore deemed endless Missouri."

West of the pass, the men were in the watershed of the Columbia, but exactly where, they did not know, for the country was contorted with ridges and mountains through which fell deep ravines and streams. Then, on August 13, Lewis's patrol saw Indians and a dog, but they fled. Lewis set out in pursuit, unfurling an American flag, laying down his rifle, and shouting out "*tab-ba-bone, tab-ba-bone.*" "We had not continued our rout more than a mile," he wrote, "when we were so fortunate as to meet with three female savages." One of the women fled, but an old woman and a girl remained, seated on the ground, their heads bowed, "as if reconciled to die." Lewis pulled the old woman to her feet, stripped off his sleeve to show his white skin, and repeated the "*tab-ba-bone*" message. A few beads, moccasin awls, looking glasses, and some paint made more sense and calmed the anxious women.

Lewis and his men set out with their new friends and had gone but a couple of miles when sixty armed men, all mounted on horses, swept toward them. This was a

"Passed over Several high ruged Knobs and Several dreans & Springs passing to the right, & passing on the ridge devideing the waters of two Small rivers. road excessively bad . . . ." William Clark, September 17, 1805

Left: Devil's Chair, a feature on the Lolo Trail, Idaho

17

moment for mettle and Lewis summoned it. He dropped his gun and left his men, seized the American flag, and walked toward the Shoshone warriors. The women showed the presents they had received and appeared to assure the men that these visitors were good people. With this information, the Shoshones got off their horses. Lewis vividly described the encounter: "these men then advanced and embraced me very affectionately in their way which is by puting their left arm over you[r] wright sholder clasping your back, while they apply their left cheek to yours and frequently vociforate the word ah'hi-e, ah-hi-e that is, I am much pleased, I am much rejoiced."

Fate seemed to play their way at this pivotal moment for the expedition. Lewis found the Shoshones in starving condition. Drouillard and Shields killed two deer and one antelope, welcome food for the large number of people. Lewis was deeply disturbed by the ravenous appetites of the Shoshones and wrote: "I viewed these poor starved devils with pity and compassion." As a token of appreciation, the band's leader presented Lewis's patrol with tippets, elegant garments of fur and white ermine pelts which they draped over their shoulders. To affirm their appreciation and bonding in the tenuous circumstances, Lewis put on the tippet. "The men followed my example," he wrote, "and we were so[o]n completely metamorphosed." With his sunburned skin and disheveled hair, Lewis felt he had become "a complete Indian in appearance."

Lewis was stalling. He desperately needed Clark and the main party to come into view. He needed even more the translation services of Charbonneau and Sacagawea. He paid a price for having pressed on ahead. To try to hold the confidence of the Shoshones, Lewis gave the chief his gun. His men, in violation of army regulations, did the same, but circumstances clearly were not usual. The success of the expedition hinged on the actions he was taking. Lewis and the Shoshones then settled down for a night, but many of the young Indians chose to sleep in the willows far away from the fire in fear of an enemy attack. "My mind was in reallity quite as gloomy all this evening as the most affrighted Indian," wrote Lewis. The next morning, with no sign of Clark, Lewis played other cards. He told the Shoshones that a woman of their tribe was in Clark's party. He attempted to dazzle them with descriptions of the merchandise he was willing to trade for their horses. He told them of a man, Clark's servant York, who was black and had short, curly hair. He was delaying, hoping and praying that Clark would come up the river. He had to hold the Shoshones at bay, for if they bolted, his prospect of securing horses would be dashed.

On August 17 William Clark and the main contingent of the expedition came into view. The party's arrival gave much relief to Lewis, who had been chafing at the poor communications, the edginess of the Shoshones about his presence and intentions, and his eagerness to obtain horses. To the intense interest of all, Sacagawea recognized some of the people. The chief with whom Lewis had so ardently hoped to establish relations was Cameahwait, her brother. She also found that one of the other women taken captive at Three Forks had escaped the Minetarees and made her way back to the tribe. Sacagawea seemed overjoyed at finding her old friend.

The reality of leaving the Missouri, obtaining horses, and moving forward in their quest for the Pacific energized the Corps of Discovery. The party took out their canvas sails, erected a sun shade, and held a council with Cameahwait. "The chief thanked us for friendship towards himself and nation," wrote Lewis, "& declared his wish to serve us in every rispect." To cement relationships, the captains distributed peace medals, face paints, knives, awls, beads, tobacco, and looking glasses. "Every article about us appeared to excite astonishment in the[i]r minds," noted Lewis. The appearance of the men in the party (especially York), the weaponry, the dugouts with which they had ascended the Jefferson and Beaverhead, and even the "segacity" of Lewis's Newfoundland dog held the attention of the Shoshones.

Confidence was high. The captains dubbed the place Camp Fortunate. With renewed animation, Clark set out with eleven men, baggage, and axes to cross the

"The Mountains which we passed to day much worst than yesterday the last excessively bad & Thickly Strowed with falling timber & Pine Spruc fur Hackmatak & Tamerack, Steep & Stoney our men and horses much fatigued. . . ."
William Clark,
September 14, 1805
Above: Newfoundland dog

Right: On the Lochsa River near DeVoto Grove, Idaho

pass. His plan was to proceed but a few miles, fell trees, make dugouts, and prepare for the swift journey to the west by water. While Clark proceeded ahead, Lewis remained among the Shoshones to barter for horses. The fate of the expedition hinged on the enterprise of both men.

Lewis spent freely. He peddled uniform coats, leggings, handkerchiefs, knives, and beads for the horses. He assigned men to go some distance from the camp and prepare a cache. Skilled in secreting goods, they dug a hole, carried away and distributed the earth, lined the pit, and stashed scientific specimens collected above the Great Falls and vital materials the party would need during its return journey. The men sank the dugouts and pirogues with heavy stones in the stream. The strategy was to preserve the vessels from fire and flood for use during the return to St. Louis. The expedition members carried out their labors covertly, for the goal was to provide no temptation to the Shoshones to plunder either the cached supplies or the watercraft.

The days of mid-August were busy and productive, but Lewis, ever contemplative, obviously struggled with himself. He poured into his journal pages of ethnographic observations, detailed and almost desperate, to fill the empty hours. While he wrestled with his uncelebrated birthday and the meaning of life, the men broke up packing cases and canoe paddles, stretched hides over the wooden pieces, and created saddles for the horseback journey. There were no idle moments. At night the Shoshone women were available. Lewis commented on the liaisons: "to prevent this mutual exchange of good offices altogether I know it impossible to effect, particularly on the part of our young men whom some months abstanence have made very polite to those tawney damsels."

Clark's party moved ahead. The explorers encountered other Shoshones. "Those Indians," Clark wrote, "are mild in their disposition appear Sincere in their friendship, punctial, and decided. kind with what they have, to Spare." They were an object of his sympathy, for they were exceedingly poor except for their horses, preyed upon by their enemies, and on the verge of starvation in their mountainous retreat. West of the pass, Clark and his men had entered the headwaters of the Salmon River. As Clark worked his way down its banks, he discovered that they narrowed. The cliffs edged toward the river, then into it. The stream spilled "over immence rocks" and wended its way along "lofty precipces." It surged through narrows too deep to ford. "My guide and maney other Indians tell me," Clark wrote, "that the Mountains Close and is a perpendicular Clift on each Side, and Continues for a great distance and that the water runs with great violence from one rock to the other on each Side foaming and roreing thro rocks in every direction." The route to the Columbia did not lie along the Salmon. The Corps of Discovery would have to follow the Continental Divide to the north and find another watershed to get through the mountains.

As Clark sorted out the convoluted geography, Lewis set out from Camp Fortunate with nine horses and a mule that he had traded for, and two hired horses. All were heavily laden with supplies, as were a number of Indian women hired as porters. They carried clothing, canvas tenting, a traveling library, scientific instruments, herbarium sheets and paper, journals, "portable" (dehydrated) soup, cooking kettles, utensils, axes, weapons, gunpowder, trade goods, medical supplies, presentation medals for chiefs, and personal possessions. "I had now the inexpressible satisfaction to find myself once more under way with all my baggage and party," wrote Lewis.

The joy that surged through Lewis and his men was not felt by Clark, who was coping with the difficulties of the mountains. The trail was barely passable. Clark slipped on the rocks and badly bruised his leg. "Every man appeared disheartened from the prospects of the river, and nothing to eat," he wrote. When the party ate chokecherries and red hawthorn berries, the men became sick. Dew collected at night, wetting the blankets. Clark sent a note back to Lewis laying out the options. First was to "proceed on by land to Some navagable part of the *Columbia River*, or to the *Ocean*." Second was for part of the expedition to try to descend the Salmon, while the remainder tried a land route

"I determined to halt the next day rest our horses and take some scelestial Observations." Meriwether Lewis, September 9, 1805

Left: Lolo Creek at Lolo Pass, Idaho

21

and, from time to time, descended into the canyon to meet those on the river. Third was for a party to fall back to the Missouri and try to push west via the Madison River.

The water route mentality permeated the thinking of the captains. Perhaps it was the long ascent of the Missouri that so fixed in their minds the transit of the American West as an experiment in river navigation. Maybe it was Jefferson's instruction to find "the most direct and practicable water communication across this continent" that bedeviled their thinking. High in the Rockies, indeed but a few miles from the great divide of watersheds, Clark was still thinking about water travel, for he wrote: "I saw Several trees which would make Small Canoes and by putting 2 together would make a Siseable one."

Circumstances compelled the Corps of Discovery to try to find the route traveled by the Nez Perce in their transit of the mountains to the Great Plains. Cameahwait told Lewis that such a route lay to the north, but explained that it was bad. He said that travelers were subjected to cold, rocks, fallen timber, and an almost total absence of game. The Nez Perce trail became the leaders' new objective. They turned north and sought the Bitterroot Valley of western Montana.

The mountains exacted their toll. They were high, rocky, and heavily forested. The horses slipped and fell. The last thermometer broke in an accident. Snow fell, followed by a cold, miserable rain. Crippled horses, hungry men, worsening weather, and uncertainty about the route plagued the party. Events turned on September 4 when the Corps of Discovery surmounted a divide and, after proceeding a number of miles, entered a village of nearly four hundred Flathead Indians. They had thirty-three lodges, eighty warriors, and more than five hundred horses. The meeting was friendly, the Indians throwing their robes over the shoulders of the weary travelers and offering to smoke in peace. Although there was little to eat, the exploring party camped with the Flatheads, smoking the pipe and talking long into the evening. "I was the first white man who ever wer[e] on the waters of this river," wrote an exultant William Clark.

The encounter with the Flathead Indians proved fortuitous, for it afforded the Corps of Discovery the opportunity to barter for more horses. Lewis and Clark distributed presidential peace medals, tobacco, and small gifts to the chiefs. In turn the tribal leaders presented berries, roots, goat and antelope skins, and the pelts of the badger and otter. For four days the expedition moved down the Bitterroot Valley. The hunters scoured the hills for game, killing an elk, deer, prairie fowl, and three geese. Food was insufficient for the hungry party.

On September 9 the men reached the mouth of Lolo Creek; the leaders named the site "Travelers' Rest." A clear, cold stream running down out of the mountains to the west, Travelers' Rest Creek was the gateway to the western ridges. Lewis and Clark decided to lay over. They wanted to take observations to try to establish the longitude and latitude of their position, and give the hunters time to bag more game. The captains were mindful of the ominous warnings about the Lolo Trail. Food was already scarce, and to tempt the mountains without any reserve supplies seemed foolhardy indeed.

While camped at this point, Clark traveled a dozen miles farther down the valley and discovered the Clark Fork, a major tributary of the upper Columbia. The party now realized that the Clark Fork was a potential shortcut either to Three Forks or to the Great Falls of the Missouri. Had they abandoned the Missouri at the Great Falls and headed toward the Clark Fork country, they might have shortened their expedition by as much as sixty or seventy days. But such considerations were hindsight. Travelers' Rest was a place of sobering geographical realities. Four deer, four ducks, and three prairie fowl did little to prepare for the trip ahead.

Accompanied by Flathead guides as well as Old Toby, a Shoshone guide, the party began its ascent of Lolo Creek on September 10. The trip consumed four days.

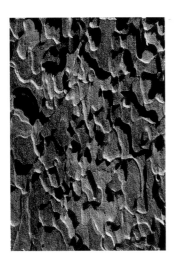

"On this roade & particularly on this Creek the Indians have pealed a number of Pine for the under bark which they eate at certain Seasons of the year, I am told in the Spring they make use of this bark . . . ." William Clark, September 12, 1805
Above: Ponderosa pine (Pinus ponderosa) observed on October 1, 1805, on Clearwater River near Orofino, Idaho

"Killed 4 deer & 4 Ducks & 3 prarie fowls. day fair Wind N.W." William Clark, September 9, 1805
Right: Pond at Star Meadows, upper Lochsa River, Idaho

Overleaf: White water on the upper Lochsa River, Idaho

The route wandered from marshy and brush-filled bottoms along the creek to sidehills covered with tangles of fallen pines. Evidence of hungry traveling parties abounded, for the men could see where Indians had hacked away the bark of living pine trees to get to the cambium layer, which they ate when starving.

Lolo Hot Springs was one of the special features of this route. Bubbling out of the ground, the springs were popular with elk, deer, and Indians, who had dug a soaking pool fed by the hot flow. "I put my finger in the water," wrote Clark, and "at first could not bare it in a Second." The expedition pressed on through quagmires of beaver dams and fallen pine saplings, until finally on September 13 it arrived at Packer Meadows. Ancient beaver ponds, filled with silt, had assumed the appearance of a landscape of small greens, surrounded by handsome stands of pine and larch. The expedition moved through the meadows to Glade Creek and settled down to eat a few pheasants and a solitary deer. Snow-covered mountains surrounded this camp at the summit of Lolo Pass.

The Indian trail led alluringly west and downhill. The men and horses descended to the Lochsa River. The route was familiar to the Flatheads, who had discovered that they could catch salmon—not available in the Bitterroot Valley—if they traversed Lolo Pass to the Lochsa. Lewis and Clark found their two large fishing weirs. The Indians' horses had cropped off nearly all the grass. The Corps of Discovery had to move on, dropping two miles farther downstream. Hungry and weary in the descent from the pass, the men killed a colt for dinner and dubbed the rivulet Kilt Colt Creek.

The upper Lochsa was magnificent country. Drenched in rain falling from the clouds confronting the high elevation of the pass to the east, the land was covered with conifers. Majestic cedars, their fibrous bark ribbed and weathered gray, grew in the bottoms along Crooked Creek and the Lochsa. On the hillsides were brilliant-hued larch, turning from green to yellow with the dropping temperatures and coming of winter. The larches stood among Englemann spruce, their short limbs spiraling symmetrically around their trunks like tens of thousands of cultured Christmas trees. Douglas fir, lodgepole pine, whitebark pine, and grand fir also clothed the hillsides. The forest was a mosaic of old growth and slopes filled with snags and underbrush where lightning strikes had ignited the forest and plunged it into an orgy of revegetation.

Lewis and Clark were hopeful that the Lochsa—known to the Indians as the Koos-koos-kee River—would take them west. Their hopes were shattered a few miles below Kilt Colt Creek when the canyon narrowed and the Indian trail played out. The Lochsa, like the Salmon River, plunged from the small valley near its headwaters into a deepening canyon with sheer rock walls. There was only one way to go and that way was almost straight up.

At Wendover Ridge the Corps of Discovery turned north, leaving the Lochsa to ascend nearly two thousand feet. The men staggered, stumbled, and pressed on with growing fatigue. The horses slipped, fell, and rolled down the steep hills. One, carrying Clark's treasured writing desk and small trunk, careened more than forty yards down the mountainside and stopped only because it lodged against a tree. The accident smashed Clark's desk, but his horse escaped mostly unhurt. On the night of September 15 the weary party reached the top. "From this mountain I could observe high ruged mountains in every direction as far as I could See," wrote Clark. Ahead lay nearly ninety miles of ridges—the awesome Bitterroots—and east nearly twenty miles lay Lolo Pass. The missteps from Glade Creek to the Lochsa and out of the drainage to the high country had consumed the energy of the men and deteriorated the condition of the horses. Bone tired, the party struggled to find water and cooked the remains of the colt and two pheasants for dinner.

"The *Snow* began to fall about 3 hours before Day," wrote Clark on September 16. The snowfall was continuous, laying down a blanket of white on the mountains, the forest, and the trail. The thick conifers poured wet snow down onto the men as they passed. Keeping warm and heading in the right direction were essential to survival. The

"I found a Spring and halted for the rear to come up and to let our horses rest & feed, about 2 hours the rear of the party came up much fatigued & horses more So, Several horses Sliped and roled down Steep hills which hurt them verry much   The one which Carried my desk & Small trunk Turned over & roled down a mountain for 40 yards & lodged against a tree, broke the Desk the horse escaped and appeared but little hurt . . . ." Willam Clark, September 15, 1805

Left: Ascent to Saddle Camp, Bitterroot Mountains, Idaho

27

Corps of Discovery had arrived at the severest of threats to existence: hunger, confusion, waning energy, and endless miles of ridges and switchbacks over a trail buried in snowfall. Clark took one man and hurried ahead of the main party about six miles to lay large warming fires, both to mark the way and to restore the weary travelers to life. No one commented on Sacagawea and how she fared with her infant son in these conditions; perhaps all took it as a matter of course. The travelers found a narrow bottom below a ridge, barely large enough with level ground to hold the wet, cold, hungry men. That night they killed a second colt on which "all Suped hartily," and, Clark noted, "thought it fine meat."

The next morning the crew awakened to find the horses had scattered; some men had to backtrack to look for the vital mounts. The snow continued to fall off the trees, wetting everyone and everything. Departure was deferred until 1:00 P.M. and then the route taken was not long. The party camped near a singular place on the trail, the Sinque Hole. A colt again "fell a Prey" to the party's appetites. The road remained difficult. The demands of the mountains had shoved the Corps of Discovery to the brink. On September 18 the captains split up. Clark set out ahead with six men; his goal was to travel as fast and far as possible to try to break free of the Bitterroots and find food for those still on the trail. Lewis and the remaining personnel covered eighteen miles. They were reduced to a wretched diet: "a skant proportion of portable soupe," bear oil, and tallow candles. "The first," wrote Lewis, "is but a poor dependance in our present situation where there is nothing upon earth ex[c]ept ourselves and a few small pheasants, small grey Squirrels, and a blue bird of the vulter kind . . . used snow for cooking."

Clark moved fast. His patrol covered thirty-six miles and camped at Hungry Creek, aptly named in light of the circumstances. At Sherman Peak a break in the weather gave the men the first view of what lay beyond the mountains. On the far horizon stretched open meadows. When Lewis's party spied the same vista the following day, Lewis wrote: "to our inexpressable joy discovered a large tract of Prairie country lying to the S. W. and widening as it appeared to extend to the W." Troubles plagued the party. Through negligence, Alexander Willard lost his horse. Robert Frazer's horse fell and tumbled nearly one hundred yards down the mountain into a creek. To the astonishment of all, when its packs were removed, the horse rose, shook itself, and in twenty minutes, was reloaded and back on the trail. "This was the most wonderfull escape I ever witnessed," wrote Lewis.

Cold, hunger, trees across the trail, lost horses—these were more than sufficient tests; yet the Bitterroots offered more. Lewis's men suffered from boils and dysentery. Perhaps both were a consequence of poor hygiene. Certainly the diet—which on some evenings was a candle for supper—did little to nurture good health. Yet, in spite of all adversity—including the loss of Lewis's winter clothing through the straying of a pack horse—the mission continued.

On September 20, nearly starving, Lewis engaged in a remarkable flurry of ornithology. First he described the varied thrush. Next he saw a Steller's jay, a bird with brilliant blue feathers and a tuft of jet-black feathers on its head; "it's note is cha-ah, cha-ah," he wrote. He observed a gray jay and a black woodpecker, the latter ultimately known as Lewis's woodpecker. Then he described three "species of Pheasants," actually the blue grouse, spruce grouse, and Oregon ruffled grouse. Perhaps Lewis was staving off despair and hunger as he penned the lines about these wonderful birds. Maybe he was just rising to President Jefferson's expectations.

That same day Clark pressed on ahead, as he phrased it, "through a Countrey as ruged as usial." His detachment had entered the western foothills of the Bitterroots, a terrain fractured by the ravines of Eldorado and Lolo Creeks but opening, at last, into level country. Clark explained that he "proceeded on through a butifull Countrey for three miles to a Small Plain" and there he found a late summer camp of

"Passed much falling timber this Mountain is covered with Spruce & Pitch pine fir, & what is called Northard Hackmatrack & Tamerack . . . ."
William Clark,
September 14, 1805
Right: Western larch
(Larix occidentalis) noted by
Lewis June 16, 1806,
Bitterroot Mountains, Idaho

Nez Perce. He first encountered three boys who, when they saw him, ran and hid in the grass. He dismounted, passed his gun to one of his men, and found two of the boys. He gave them small pieces of ribbon and sent them off to the village. This was a pivotal moment of first contact. Never before had Euro-Americans penetrated the vast homeland of the Nez Perce. Safe transit through their lands depended on establishing good relations.

The Nez Perce, though cautious, welcomed the strangers. They gave the famished men buffalo meat, dried salmonberries and roots, and bread made from camas or *pas-shi-co*. Clark's party had entered Weippe Prairie, a tableland of hundreds of acres of camas fields at the margin of the forested Bitterroots. From time immemorial the Nez Perce had gathered there to dig and bake the bulbs. Camas was the staff of life to the tribe and many of their neighbors. These people, identified by Clark as the "Cho pun-nish," were friendly. Clark found that trade goods had already reached this remote hinterland of the continent: the Nez Perce had blue and white glass beads and pieces of brass and copper.

Lewis and the main body of the expedition moved on through the forests along Eldorado Creek. They ate what they could find: grouse, a coyote, a horse, and crayfish from the creek. The scavenging "enabled us to make one more hearty meal," wrote Lewis, "not knowing where the next was to be found." The forest rose in splendor around the party. Lewis saw majestic cedars "large enough to form eligant perogues of at least 45 feet in length." The lure of water travel continued to engage his imagination. The reality of his situation grumbled in his stomach. "I find myself growing weak for want of food," he wrote, "and most of the men complain of a similar deficiency and have fallen off very much."

Two days later, on September 22, Lewis was yet beset with troubles on the trail. In spite of precise instructions to hobble horses, one of the men had proven neglectful and the horses had wandered off, an event delaying the party until almost midday. A couple of hours later, however, prospects improved, for Lewis's party met Reuben Fields, who had been sent out by Clark to carry food to the beleaguered travelers. Fields brought dried berries, roots, fish, a crow, and news that the Nez Perce were but eight miles ahead. Lewis halted the contingent for a luncheon of crow and Indian foodstuffs. Then the men proceeded on through the forests, which changed mostly to pine. Lewis sensed victory and release as he entered Weippe Prairie:

> the pleasure I now felt in having tryumphed over the rocky Mountains and decending once more to a level and fertile country where there was every rational hope of finding a comfortable subsistence for myself and party can be more readily conceived than expressed, nor was the flattering prospect of the final success of the expedition less pleasing.

The challenge of the mountains had been all that the Missouri had exacted from the Corps of Discovery and then some. At least in the ascent of the Missouri the captains had a sense of where they were headed and dependable supplies of food. Once they had abandoned their vessels on the Beaverhead and set out by land, their journey had become less and less certain. The mountains had enforced privation in both food shortages and weather conditions, and had inflicted extreme physical and mental punishments, sapping the strength of man and beast and trying the souls of the two captains. A realization fixed itself in their minds, that the window of opportunity for getting over the rest of the Bitterroots was short, perhaps a matter of a few weeks, maybe a month or two. Were they to return the way they had come, they would face again the tests of these almost endless ridges. A region mostly devoid of game and a landscape of repetitive meandering ridges was not an easy prospect to carry, but it became a new part of the mental baggage of the Corps of Discovery. Ahead lay more adventures and, hopefully, a swift run to the sea.

"At 12 miles decended the mountain to a leavel pine Countrey   proceeded on through a butifull Countrey for three miles to a Small Plain in which I found maney Indian lodges . . . ." William Clark, September 20, 1805

Left: October on the Lochsa River, Idaho

"These Savages are now laying up food for the winter and in the Spring they are going over on the medicine River and Missourie River to hunt the buffalow."

John Ordway among the Nez Perce, September 23, 1805

Above: Buffalo, source of life and inspiration to the Indians of the High Plains

"The want of provisions together with the dificuelty of passing those emence mountains dampened the Spirits of the party which induced us to Some plan of reviving ther Sperits. I deturmined to take a party of the hunters and proceed on in advance to Some leavel Country . . . ." William Clark, September 18, 1805

Right: Fall colors at daylight, Bald Peak, Bitterroot Mountains, Idaho

"I tasted this water and found it hot & not bad tasted . . . .
in further examonation I found this water nearly boiling hot
at the places it Spouted from the rocks . . . .   I put my finger
in the water, at first could not bare it in a Second—"

William Clark, September 13, 1805

Left: Hot mineral water, Warm Springs Creek, upper Lochsa River, Idaho

Above: View east from Bald Peak in the Bitterroot Mountains, Idaho

"I found great dificulty in finding the road in the evining as the Snow had fallen
from 6 to 8 Inches deep, verry Cold and the pine which in maney places verry thick
So covered with Snow, as in passing I became wet . . . ." William Clark, September 16, 1805

Overleaf: Ridge of the Bitterroot Mountains west of Papoose Saddle, Idaho

Crossing the Columbia Plateau

"The *Cho-pun-nish* or Pierced nose Indians are Stout likely men, handsom women, and verry dressey in their way, the dress of the men are a white Buffalow robe or Elk Skin dressed with Beeds which are generally white, Sea Shells—i e Mother of Pirl hung to ther hair & on a pice of otter Skin about their necks hair Cewed in two parsels hanging forward over their Sholders, feathers, and different Coloured Paints which they find in their Countrey Generally white, Green & light Blue."

William Clark, October 10, 1805

The Corps of Discovery found a receptive audience among the Nez Perce. These people of the high plains and river canyons west of the mountains had heard about white men. Their homeland was expansive: Nez Perce bands resided in the Wallowa and Grand Ronde watershed of northeastern Oregon, on the lower reaches of Hells Canyon on the Snake and the Salmon, and in the Selway, Lochsa, and Clearwater drainages in north-central Idaho. Some Nez Perce also hunted and gathered on the grasslands above the Snake in southeastern Washington. The people were reserved but curious.

Nez Perce women wore glass and brass beads that had passed through the hands of traders in a transit of hundreds of miles in the aboriginal trade network. A woman among them had lived with the Minatarees, had seen white men, and spoke favorably of them. Conditions appeared promising for cordial relations—and the expedition needed all the friendly support it could get.

Clark and the advance patrol played a careful strategy at Weippe Prairie. They tarried to trade for foodstuffs and secure geographical information, while chafing to get to the river to the west. Patience proved important, for they had to allay any suspicion among the Nez Perce that their intentions might be hostile. The days were warm; the trade was brisk. Clark purchased meager supplies and dispatched Reuben Fields east over the trail to find Lewis's party. The missions accomplished, Clark and his men moved several miles and descended to the river.

The Clearwater was a majestic stream, dark green, cold, swift, and swirling in troubled moods. Fed by the Lochsa and Selway, it drained mountains, forests, and ravines; winter snows and spring rains dumped by Pacific storm systems ensured steady runoff. Its banks were lined with towering cottonwoods whose leaves rustled in the nearly perpetual wind sweeping through the canyon. Thickets of willow, alder, ash, and Indian arrowwood nestled along the shore. Above the river rose impressive slopes where the grass was sun-dried into brown and yellow straw; the talus was laid down with tens of thousands of shattered stones; and patches of poison ivy burnished the hillsides with red leaves that hinted at coming winter.

Clark's party found tough going. The advance patrol did not make camp on the river until shortly before midnight. The Indians who lived nearby were cheerful and friendly. Clark kept up appearances, opening discussions with Twisted Hair, their leader, but coping with stomach and bowel problems. He hovered on the edge of nausea and finally succumbed to vomiting. On September 22, Lewis and the main body of travelers also reached the Clearwater and joined Clark's party.

The expedition was at another crossroads. Red meat had sustained the men for months during the ascent of the Missouri and its tributaries. Crossing the Bitterroots, however, had diminished the travelers' health. Wan from malnutrition, lethargic and nauseated by the irregular diet, and undoubtedly dispirited by the cold, wet, monotonous journey through the mountains, the men were not in a position to defend themselves. The Nez Perce, healthy, armed, well equipped with fine herds of horses, and having mastery of the terrain, were, perforce, arbiters of the passage. The survival of the expedition

Left: Nez Perce woman's dress, tanned deer hide with dentalia shells and trade beads (Nez Perce National Monument, Lapwai, Idaho)

depended on the attitudes and actions of the Nez Perce. They took no advantage; instead, they played gracious hosts, greeting, trading, and providing information by sign language to the two captains.

Lewis and Clark did their best to cement positive relations. As Clark put it, they "made 3 Chiefs" by passing out tobacco, handkerchiefs, knives, small American flags, and medals. The "peace medals" carried the image of President Washington or Jefferson on one side, and clasped hands with the words "PEACE AND FRIENDSHIP" on the reverse, just above the crossed images of a peace pipe and tomahawk. While diplomacy helped, the temperament of the Nez Perce carried the day. They were a generous people, willing to play hosts to these travelers, the likes of which had never before appeared in their homeland. They came to look at the strangers with their fancy guns, hairy faces, and different ways. They came to barter roots, camas, berries, fish, and tanned hides of elk and deer; the travelers, their clothing in tatters from the rigors of crossing the mountains, were eager to make new leather shirts and pantaloons.

The Corps of Discovery was reduced in flesh and in strength but had to press on. Clark set out to explore downstream from camp. His horse threw him three times, badly bruising his hip. Sickness spread through the camp. Lewis was debilitated, barely able to ride a gentle horse loaned by one of the chiefs. When the full party set out, some of the men lay down by the side of the trail, wracked with stomachaches and intestinal problems. Others had to be lifted to their horses. "All Complain of a *Lax* & heaviness at the Stomack," wrote Clark. He distributed Dr. Rush's Pills, the "thunderbolts" that produced almost instantaneous diarrhea. The remedy was almost worse than the symptoms!

The party traveled down the Clearwater, identified in the journals as the Kooskooskee. Lewis and Clark selected a site on the west bank opposite the entrance of the North Fork. Their "Canoe Camp" was ideal: it had good drainage and visibility. It was on the main route of Indian river travel, and thus a place for access to salmon, roots, and berries. Above all, it was surrounded by towering ponderosa pines; from these, the men planned to craft dugouts to resume their journey by water to the Pacific.

Administering salts, pills, jalap, and "tarter" emetic, the captains ordered the able men to craft handles for the axes and start felling trees to build canoes. The axes were small for the large task but, as was repeatedly the case, the men had no alternative but to persevere. They began a ten-day marathon of designing, chopping, hewing, and crafting their vessels. Five long dugout canoes began to take shape on the banks of the Clearwater. The warm, sultry weather was a respite from the cold of the mountains, but the men remained sick. Provisions were scarce; the hunters had little luck in the nearby mountains. "Nothing to eate but dried roots and Dried fish," wrote Clark. "Capt. Lewis and my Self eate a Supper of roots boiled, which filled us So full of wind, that we were Scercely able to Breathe all night felt the effects of it."

On October 5 Lewis ordered the men to brand the mark "U.S. Capt. M. Lewis" on thirty-eight horses. They also cropped the foretop of the mane "that we may be able to know them on our return," wrote Joseph Whitehouse. By careful arrangement and adroit communication via sign language, the captains lined up three Nez Perce men to take charge of their livestock. They offered each a knife and shell gorget in payment. The next day a patrol cached the party's saddles, a canister of powder, and a bag of rifle balls.

The transit from the Beaverhead to Canoe Camp had consumed just over seven weeks and had defied Jefferson's fondest hopes of a short and easy water route for the commerce of Asia to flow into the heartland of North America. On October 7 the men loaded their craft and set out. The Corps of Discovery was again moving by water, but this time westward, down the great river system of the Columbia. Hope revived, even as the men nursed sore bellies and bowels.

The Clearwater carried the Corps twenty miles through ten rapids. In the third riffle the lead dugout struck a rock and began leaking. The remedy was to unload and

Above: Jefferson peace medal (Roger W. Wendlick Collection, Portland, Oregon)

"The pleasure I now felt in having tryumphed over the rocky Mountains and decending once more to a level and fertile country where there was every rational hope of finding a comfortable subsistence for myself and party can be more readily conceived than expressed, nor was the flattering prospect of the final success of the expedition less pleasing."
Meriwether Lewis,
September 22, 1805

Right: Vicinity of Canoe Camp, Clearwater River, Idaho

patch the thin place. This day the captains selected a landmark snag to cache two lead canisters of powder. The strategic establishment of caches, even small ones such as this, enabled the recovery of critically needed supplies during the return journey.

On the second day the expedition ran fifteen rapids, none too difficult, and skirted four islands. Sixteen miles downstream, the canoe bearing Sergeant Patrick Gass and his party split open along one side. Several of the men could not swim but had presence of mind to hang onto the gunwales. Rescuers pulled them out and salvaged the wet cargo. The only thing to do was to open the packages, post sentinels to keep away the eager hands of visiting Indians, and dry the goods. The process took the following day and a second night at the unanticipated campsite.

At this point the expedition was nearly forty miles downstream from Canoe Camp. This realization perhaps proved too much for the Shoshone guides, or maybe it was the hiring of two Nez Perce chiefs to help direct the party through their homeland. Without their promised pay, the Shoshone men fled east. "We requested the Chief to Send a horseman after our old guide to come back and recive his pay," wrote Clark, but the chief advised against the effort. He pointed out that the Nez Perce would likely relieve the former guides of any goods before they got to the mountains.

While at this camp, the travelers had a singular experience. An Indian woman visited them and gave away all her possessions. Working herself into a state, she "would Scarrify her Self in a horid manner," observed Clark. Gass wrote that the woman exhibited a "crazy fit, and cut her arms from the wrists to the shoulders, with a flint" and that her people had great trouble calming her. While this woman may have suffered from derangement, it is also possible that she was a particular type of shaman. Among the Nez Perce these were temperamental figures opposed to disruption and disorder. If one of these shamans saw and liked some object, the best action was to yield it, otherwise the aggrieved shaman was likely to lose control, throw a tantrum, curse the owner of the object, and even engage in self-mutilation.

Every few miles the travelers found an Indian village, fishing site, or camp, either on the shore or on islands. Lodges, huts, sweat lodges, and fish-drying racks were evidence of human presence. Their health returning and their spirits soaring with the ease of river travel, the explorers were intensely hungry. On October 10 they purchased six dogs; on October 11, seven. Dog meat, not salmon, climbed to preferred status in the diet of the party. "Most of our people having been accustomed to meat," wrote Patrick Gass, "do not relish the fish, but prefer dog meat; which, when well cooked, tastes very well."

Sixty miles from Canoe Camp the Corps of Discovery reached the confluence of the Clearwater and the Snake, denominated "Lewis's River" on their maps. Unlike the crystal clear Kooskooskee, the Snake was deep bluish green. "Indians continue all day on the banks to view us as low as the forks," wrote Clark. The night was warm, but clouds rolled in and obscured the moon, prohibiting lunar observations to try to fix the precise location of the junction of the rivers. Charbonneau, never a man to fit in well with any group, got into a general misunderstanding with Joseph and Reuben Fields, something that arose from a jest but led to hurt feelings.

The lower Snake cut through layers of ancient basalt flows. Pouring like taffy out of great crevices in the earth, molten basalt had flowed in slow waves, filled in low places and, over millions of years, created the generally level appearance of the Columbia Plateau. Streams like the Snake and Columbia carved their courses through these layers. The exposed faces of rock were subject to weathering by wind and freeze-shattering. They stood like great stacked layer cakes above the rivers. Slopes of talus spilled down the hillsides toward the streambanks.

The Corps of Discovery floated through these scenes of stark grandeur. Most of the Nez Perce and Palouse who lived in this region were on the plains hunting for antelope. Contact almost inevitably led to barter for foodstuffs: dogs and dried fish. The presence of Sacagawea was taken as a good sign by the people who lived in the small villages.

"Those people were glad to See us & gave us drid Sammon one had formerly been taken by the Minitarries of the north & seen white men, our guide called the Chief who was fishing on the other Side of the river, whome I found a Cherfull man of about 65 I gave him a Medal." William Clark, September 21, 1805

Left: Nez Perce canoe (Edward S. Curtis)

Above: Clouds above the Clearwater River near Lapwai, Idaho

"The wife of Shabono our interpetr we find reconsiles all the Indians, as to our friendly intentions a woman with a party of men is a token of peace," concluded Clark.

Downstream from the mouth of the Tucannon River, a tributary draining the Blue Mountains, a dugout swept sideways against a rock; water surged into its stern. The harried paddlers leaped from the canoe and onto the rock as the vessel sank. Bedding and packages floated away on the current. The mishap resulted in the loss of shot pouches, tomahawks, and dried roots. Everything saved was wet, including precious powder carried in an unsealed container. The canisters tied to the bottom of the canoe were saved, but many valued possessions were lost.

The travelers stopped on an island to assess their losses and lay out the wet items to dry in the sun. The captains found a cache of house boards weighted down with stones. "We have made it a point at all times not to take any thing belonging to the Indians even their wood," wrote Clark, "but at this time we are Compelled to violate that rule and take a part of the Split timber we find here bured for fire wood, as no other is to be found in any direction."

On October 15, still descending the lower Snake, the party found the country bleak and lacking firewood. Willow and hackberry grew in patches along the river. There were no trees and, above, only the vast plains of the Plateau. The explorers looted a village: "here we were obliged for the first time to take the property of the Indians without the consent or approbation of the owner," wrote Clark. "The night was cold & we made use of part of those boards and Split logs for fire wood."

The Corps of Discovery reached the Columbia on October 16. The Indians of the area had heard about them from the Nez Perce chiefs who had preceded the main flotilla. Throngs of local residents gathered to see the strangers. The captains smoked tobacco with the Indians, and then ordered their men to set up camp. A short time later a chief arrived from a nearby village, accompanied by "about 200 men Singing and beeting on their drums." They formed a half circle around the expeditionary force, singing for some time. Lewis and Clark, by sign language, attempted to explain their travels and friendly intentions. They presented medals to three chiefs. The evening grew long as the captains bartered for dogs and the chiefs returned with presents of fuel, fish, and dried horse meat.

Clark used the occasion of camping at the Snake and Columbia Rivers to write a summary of travels and observations comparable to what he wrote for the transit of the Lolo Trail and the descent of the Clearwater. A man of intense concentration and great attention to detail, he laid out the course in direction, sometimes in degrees, then miles, and finally in summary descriptive terms. He crafted a virtual windshield view of the journey in his reprise narratives. His observations covered the nature of the river, its obstacles and currents, islands, vistas of the nearby countryside, and from time to time, data on the Indian fishing scaffolds, dwellings, and cemeteries.

The river junction became the occasion to camp two nights and spend a day making observations. Lewis recorded Indian vocabularies. He used a word list prepared by Albert Gallatin and Thomas Jefferson, who hoped to settle the matter of the origin of the peoples of the Americas. Theories abounded: Indians were descended from Phoenicians, Carthaginians, Welsh fishermen, and the Lost Tribes of Israel. The word lists solicited fundamental terms such as father, mother, hand, finger, God, and eye. It was anticipated that they would facilitate comparative analysis. Sadly, the numerous compilations, including those made at this camp, were lost. (A fragment of Lewis's list of Pawnee words survives at the American Philosophical Society.)

Clark used his free day to explore the Columbia. With two men he headed upstream ten miles against the current to explore the shoreline and observe the Natives. He found numerous lodges constructed of reed matting and large scaffolds for drying fish. "The Waters of this river is Clear," wrote Clark, "and a Salmon may be Seen at the deabth of 15 or 20 feet." The fall runs were ending; hundreds of dying fish

Above: Cayuse woman with traditional hat, braids, and dress decorated with trade beads. Cayuse, ca. 1900 (Major Lee Moorhouse)

"We have made it a point at all times not to take any thing belonging to the Indians even their wood. but at this time we are Compelled to violate that rule and take a part of the Split timber we find here bured for fire wood, as no other is to be found in any direction." William Clark, October 14, 1805

Right: Snake River cutting through the Plateau near Clarkston, Washington

lay in the spawning areas and along the banks. The Natives were busily engaged in preserving vital food supplies for the coming winter. Clark stopped to visit a village and described the warm hospitality he encountered:

> one of those Mat lodges I entered found it crouded with men women and children and near the enterance of those houses I saw maney Squars engaged Splitting and drying Salmon. I was furnished with a mat to Sit on, and one man Set about prepareing me Something to eate, first he brought in a piece of a Drift log of pine and with a wedge of the elks horn, and a malet of Stone curioesly Carved he Split the log into Small pieces and lay'd it open on the fire on which he put round Stones, a woman handed him a basket of water and a large Salmon about half Dried, when the Stones were hot he put them into the basket of water with the fish which was Soon Sufficiently boiled for use. it was then taken out put on a platter of rushes neetly made, and Set before me they boiled a Salmon for each of the men with me.

The explorers wrote positively about the Yakamas and Wanapams. They admired their hard work processing fish, and described their personal decorations of shell, feather, bone, brass, copper, and horn. "Those people appears to live in a State of comparitive happiness," observed Clark, noting that both men and women shared in labor and that monogamy appeared to prevail. "Those people respect the aged with veneration," he wrote. "I observed an old woman in one of the Lodges which I entered She was entirely blind as I was informed by Signs, had lived more than 100 winters, She occupied the best position in the house, and when She spoke great attention was paid to what She Said."

Before resuming their journey the explorers measured the width of the rivers at their confluence. They found the Snake 575 yards wide and the Columbia 960 3/4 yards across. They attempted to establish their location. "Took a meridian altitude 68° 57′ 30″ the Suns upper Limb. The Latitudes produced is 46° 15′ 13 9/10″ North," recorded Clark. And from an important chief, *Cutssahnim*, they secured a sketch of the Columbia upstream on which they recorded the numbers of villages.

These tasks completed, the Corps resumed its downriver journey at 4:00 P.M. on October 18. In twenty-one miles, the party entered Wallula Gap. At this point the Columbia makes a sharp turn, cutting deep into the uprising basalt. A mixture of sand and dust sometimes clouds the air and blasts everything and everyone in its path in the gap. The setting is moody, twisted by the change in the course of the river. On the south shore stand twin pinnacles of eroded basalt that have resisted the surges of calamitous floods, such as those pouring out of ancient Lake Missoula and slamming through Wallula Gap on their way to the sea, some twelve thousand years ago.

In spite of its arid and treeless setting, the course of the river was well populated. Natives occupied almost every island of any size and viewed the travelers with great curiosity and sometimes fear. The journals became a tally of Indian lodges, fishing scaffolds, drying racks, islands, and rapids. The captains handed out medals and beads, made new friends, and smoked with tribal leaders. Pierre Cruzatte and George Gibson entertained the guests by playing the violin, while the men ate some of the forty dogs they had purchased at the forks of the Snake and Columbia.

The disorientation produced by the intrusion of the expedition into the homeland of the Cayuse and Umatillas was evident in an incident on October 19. Clark, no fan of dog meat dinners, eagerly hunted for gulls, ducks, geese, and other birds. "While Setting on a rock wateing for Capt. Lewis," he wrote, "I shot a Crain which was flying over." The action of bringing a bird out of the sky with the production of a loud explosion was witnessed by several Indians who fled to their lodges. Concerned that they may have interpreted his actions as hostile, Clark hurried to their village to allay their fears. He found the village deserted but, opening one lodge, he counted thirty-two men, women, and children cowering "in the greatest agutation,

"The Country on either Side is an open plain leavel & fertile after assending a Steep assent of about 200 feet not a tree of any kind to be Seen on the river . . . ." William Clark, October 11, 1805
Left: Sandhills on the Snake River, Washington

"S.W. 14 miles to a rock in a Lard. resembling a hat just below a rapid at the lower Point of an Island in the Midl of the river . . . ." William Clark, October 19, 1805
Above: Hat Rock on the Columbia River near Umatilla, Oregon

Some crying and ringing their hands, others hanging their heads." Clark offered gifts, took out his pipe, and dispatched his men to the other lodges to do likewise. "I then Set my Self on a rock and made Signs to the men to come and Smoke with me," he wrote. With caution and coaxing, they came forward. "They said we came from the clouds &c &c and were not men &c &c," he noted. The timely arrival of Lewis, the two Nez Perce chiefs, and Sacagawea quelled the anxiety. "This Indian woman, wife to one of our interps. confirmed those people of our friendly intentions," Clark concluded, "as no woman ever accompanies a war party of Indians in this quarter."

War was a reality on the Columbia Plateau in 1805. Occupancy of islands in the main channel of the Columbia River was not solely a function of convenience for fishing. Island life was protection against enemies, especially the raiders who thundered across the Plateau from the south. Probably the Indians of the Great Basin were the first to secure horses. Shifting from foot to horse, they gained tremendous advantage and used it to raid the food-rich villages along the Columbia River. The Northern Paiutes, who lived on the upper John Day and Deschutes Rivers, had used their new mobility to exercise dominion over an expansive area. West of the mouth of the Umatilla, the Corps of Discovery found few lodges and no residents on the south shore of the river for nearly two hundred miles. Evidence of the conflicts resounded in the local name for the Deschutes—Towarnehiooks—the river of the "enemies," referring to the Northern Paiutes who resided at its headwaters.

Near the mouth of the John Day River, John Collins treated the party to a welcome diversion. He crafted beer by fermenting dried, pulverized camas roots. The Corps had purchased quantities of this food from the Nez Perce. Aware of the dousings the stuff received during the river journey, Collins perceived that it was "frequently wet molded and Sowered" and used its fermentation to manufacture a modest round of beer.

The expedition took but four days to make a rapid transit of the Columbia from the Snake to the Deschutes. Ahead lay Celilo Falls and Five Mile Rapids. The upriver tribes suggested that white men lived at the falls, or close thereto, and that the kettles, brass beads, blankets, mariners' caps, and other trade items had come into their possession through the hands of those at the great narrows. Seventeen lodges of the "E-nee-sher Nation" lined the north bank above the falls and five large ones stood below. Here the Columbia spilled nearly forty feet, cutting channels through islands. Positioned on platforms and at key perches, men in the seasons of the fish runs wielded dipnets and gaffs to harvest tens of thousands of pounds of salmon. This fishery was the trade depot and crossroads of the Pacific Northwest interior. For thousands of years the food surpluses of the interior passed through the villages at Celilo in exchange for the canoes, paddles, shells, dried smelt, and commodities from west of the Cascade Mountains.

The falls dictated a laborious portage. A reconnaissance confirmed that the best option was to carry the goods twelve hundred yards along the north bank. The route passed over rock, gravel, and through a difficult course of two hundred yards of soft sand. The captains, mindful of the prospect of theft, selected an "ellegable Situation" at the west end of the portage as a defensible depot and began the task, assisted by local recruits using their horses, of moving all of the gear. Two men examined the south shore and discovered the canoe portage frequently used by the Indians. It enabled the party the following day to drag the dugouts around the worst of the falls.

Stored on the islands as well as around the lodges were immense quantities of salmon. The Indian women had wind-dried and pounded the flesh, packing it in baskets lined with salmon skin. "Thus preserved those fish may be kept Sound and Sweet Several years," wrote Clark. He observed that the people at the falls exported great quantities annually "to the whites people who visit the mouth of the river as well as to the nativs below."

During the portage the captains secured further information about intertribal dynamics: "no Indians reside on the S.W. side of this river for fear (as we were informed)

Above: Basalt sculpture from the Wasco-Wishram homeland, Columbia River (Maryhill Museum, Maryhill, Washington)

"I heard a great roreing. I landed at the Lodges and the natives went with me to the top of this rock which makes from the Stard. Side; from the top of which I could See the dificuelties we had to pass for Several miles below; at this place the water of this great river is compressed into a Chanel between two rocks not exceeding *forty five* yards wide and continues for a 1/4 of a mile when it again widens to 200 yards . . . ." William Clark, October 24, 1805

Right: Five Mile Rapids (United States Army Corps of Engineers)

of the Snake Indians, who are at war with the tribes on this river," wrote Clark. "They represent the Snake Indians as being verry noumerous, and resideng in a great number of villages on Towarnehiooks River."

The falls of the Columbia introduced the Corps of Discovery to one of Oregon Country's best-kept secrets—fleas! "We found at this place innumerable Quantities of fleas," wrote Joseph Whitehouse, "the ground being cover'd with them, and they were very troublesome." The following day the Corps of Discovery gave a new look to westward exploration. "Every man of the party was obliged to Strip naked dureing the time of takeing over the canoes," wrote Clark, "that they might have an oppertunity of brushing the fleas of their legs and bodies."

At the falls the explorers encountered harbor seals. Great numbers had ascended the Columbia in pursuit of salmon. Having passed through the rapids, they frolicked in the turgid water at the base of the falls, more than 150 miles from the sea. Hints of the proximity of the Pacific came in several messages: "Saw one half white child among them," noted Joseph Whitehouse. "Saw also new copper tea kittle beeds copper and a nomber of other articles which must have come from Some white trader," he concluded. The commerce of many worlds flowed through the hands of those residing at this emporium. The people of the falls dispatched obsidian, dried fish, bear grass for basketry, and slaves to the tribes to the west. By 1805 they had acquired a number of European items, products of the maritime fur trade.

Below the falls lay the Short and Long Narrows. At one place most of the men left the canoes, holding ropes to throw in case of accident, while an intrepid crew took the canoes through the swirling waters. The shore party carried the most valued possessions over this second portage, which Clark termed "passing through the gut." Again, large numbers of curious Wascos and Wishrams gathered to watch the strangers.

Rumors swirled almost as powerfully as the currents in the river. The Nez Perce guides, at the end of their area of familiarity and eager to depart for home, explained that they had learned of hostile intent of the Indians immediately to the west. They went ahead to try to explain the peaceful purposes of the expedition, then turned around for the Clearwater country. The two "faithful chiefs" had ably served the Corps of Discovery as guides and advance emissaries of the expedition. Taking no chances, the captains selected a camp on a point of rocks at the mouth of Quenett Creek (Mill Creek) on the south shore. "This Situation we Concieve well Calculated for defence, and Conveniant to hunt under the foots of the mountain to the West & S.W.," wrote Clark.

On October 26–27 the men lay over to dry their possessions and repair canoes with pitch extracted from the pines growing along Mill Creek. Lewis and Clark met local chiefs and exchanged presents. While the violin resounded through the evening air, York danced, to the great interest of the visitors. The hunters had good luck, bagging five deer, four large squirrels, a pheasant and a goose, while one man gigged a steelhead. Tensions surfaced in a cryptic journal entry by Clark: "Some words with Shabono our interpreter about his duty." Whether it was a matter of living up to his contracted duties or his responsibilities as a husband and father, Clark did not say, but the comment only further confirmed that Charbonneau was often the odd man out.

Differentials in barometric pressure between the interior and the region west of the mountains frequently generate brisk winds that sweep through the Columbia Gorge. Departure on October 28 proved difficult. A "hard wind" came up during the night and blew steadily all day. The party advanced but four miles. The following day the crew entered the eastern portals of the Gorge. On all sides the mountains towered above them. On the north shore they found Indian lodges far more permanent than those east on the Plateau. The men had cut and smoothed cedar planks and framed permanent, semi-subterranean lodges. They decorated the panels with carved and

"We purchased forty dogs for which we gave articles of little value, Such as beeds, bells, & thimbles, of which they appeard verry fond . . . ." William Clark, October 18, 1805

Left: Trade thimbles, bells, and beads and leather—detail of Klickitat wedding veil, ca. 1850 (Maryhill Museum, Maryhill, Washington)

Above: Klickitat basket of cedar root, bear grass, and leather (Maryhill Museum, Maryhill, Washington)

> "We landed and walked down accompanied by an old man
> to view the falls, and best rout for to make a portage."
>
> William Clark, October 22, 1805

Above: Silhouettes of fishermen in the maelstrom of Celilo Falls, ca. 1925 (Benjamin Gifford, Oregon Historical Society, Portland, Oregon)

Before acquisition of horses in the eighteenth century, natives of the Columbia Plateau relied on stealth and cooperation to hunt for deer and antelope. Long rows of stacked stones mark the places where generations of hunters created runways to drive game into ever-narrowing funnels. Men placed woven snares at the exit to entangle the legs of deer and antelope. Sometimes they stood ready with bow and arrow. Right: Basalt rock—game drive

painted designs of humans and animals. The villagers gave the party fish, berries, nuts, and root bread. The Corps purchased a dozen dogs and four sacks of pounded, dried fish. "We Call this the friendly Village," wrote Clark.

A short distance downstream lay Memaloose Island, largest of several "islands of the dead." Considering their prospects with the advent of winter, the captains looked over the countryside. On the south bank just below "Sepulchar Island," Clark described "a good Situation for winter quarters if game can be had." Since the Indians all lived on the north bank "for fear of the Snake Ind[ians]," good hunting in the rugged hillsides and forests appeared promising.

In twenty-two days the Corps of Discovery had crossed the Columbia Plateau. The descent from Canoe Camp by water dramatically sped the trek to the west. Although the river had demanded vigilance, its currents had served the party well. The men had killed ducks, geese, and fish; bartered for berries, roots, dried fish, and Indian bread; and consumed several dozen dogs obtained in the villages lining its banks. The Corps had passed through the lands of the Nez Perce, Palouse, Yakamas, Wanapams, Walla Wallas, Cayuse, Wishrams, and Wascos. Signs of a wider world appeared in almost every village, in the form of trade goods that had passed up the river. Surely, the sea was not far.

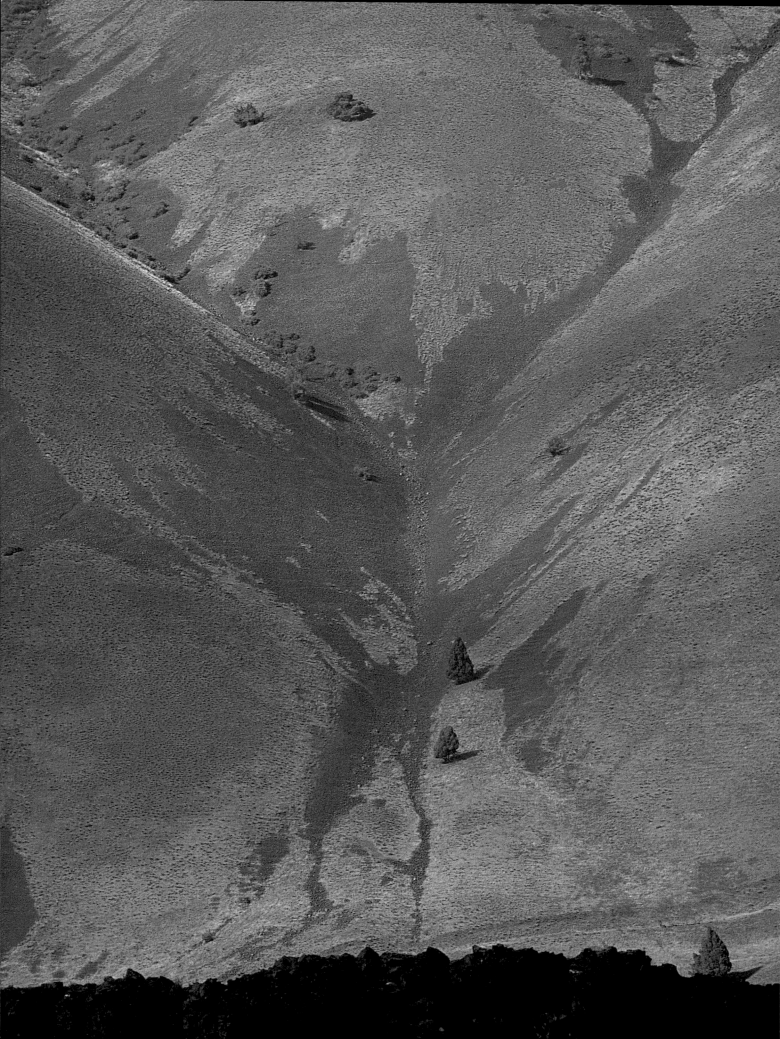

"Emence piles of rocks appears as if Sliped from
the Clifts under which they lay, passed great number
of rocks in every direction Scattered in the river"
William Clark, October 21, 1805

Left: Scablands and talus slope above John Day Dam, Washington

"On entering one of these lodges, the natives offered us a sheepkin for sail, than which
nothing could have been more acceptable except the animal itself. the skin of the head
of the sheep with the horns remaining was cased in such manner as to fit the head of a
man by whom it was woarn and highly prized as an ornament. we obtained this cap in
exchange for a knife, and were compelled to give two Elkskins in exchange for the skin."
Meriwether Lewis, April 10, 1806

Above: Mountain sheep once common along the Columbia River

From the Columbia Gorge to the Sea

"Landed at the place appointed for winters quarters . . . . we unloaded the canoes and carried all our baggage about 2 hundred yards on a rise of ground and thicket of handsom tall Strait pine and balsom fir timber and Camped here we intend to build a fort and Stay if game is to be found thro. this winter Season."

John Ordway, December 7, 1805

Chill gripped the countryside in November 1805. Driven by the bitter winds sweeping along the river, rain pelted the Corps of Discovery and gave a taste of coming winter. The trip through the Columbia Gorge carried the explorers nearly at sea level through the highest mountain range in Oregon and Washington. Carved by the currents of the Columbia and sculpted dramatically during the great Missoula Floods of the Late Pleistocene, the Gorge displayed remarkable variety and grandeur. The greatest concentration of waterfalls in North America plunged out of the forests of the high country draining the slopes of Mount Hood, and fell toward the south bank of the river. Towering rock pinnacles, quiet backwaters, frothing rapids, mysterious drowned forests, and evidence of massive landslides stimulated the curiosity of the travelers.

Below the last of the rapids was the first hint of tidewater, the head of the nearly 130-mile-long estuary of the Columbia River. The captains mounted a reconnaissance and concluded that they could not pass over the Cascades rapids with safety. They put ashore on the north bank and outfitted the men with kettles, weapons, trade goods, and personal effects to trudge over a muddy, winding trail. The route led over a forested old landslide, around boulders, into quagmires, and through ravines, passing an abandoned village, a cemetery, and another village near the Lower Cascades. Some of the party lined down the canoes, at places dragging them over rocks eight or ten feet high. "It was the most fatiguing business we have been engaged in for a long time," wrote Patrick Gass, "and we got but two over all day, the distance of about a mile." Ahead rose a monolith—rendered in Clark's inimitable spelling as "Beaten Rock." It towered nearly 850 feet above the river.

The Cascades portage was an arduous but busy trail along the north bank. While the expedition was engaged in making its journey, seven Indian women came along carrying loads of dried fish and bear grass that they had collected in the high mountains. Basketmakers to the west prized highly the shimmering strands of this grass, which they used to lay in decorative white patterns on the exteriors of their baskets. Four Indian men came down the river in a canoe loaded with pounded, dried salmon. The portage divided the Corps of Discovery: those who could not swim became burden bearers; others with ropes lowered dugouts down through the rapids.

At the Cascades, nature had asserted a strong, almost violent presence. Exactly how the place had come to be was quite mysterious. There was the "sunken forest," of which Clark wrote: "a remarkable circumstance in this part of the river is, the Stumps of pine trees are in maney places are at Some distance in the river, and gives every appearance of the rivers being damed up below from Some cause which I am not at this time acquainted with." Clark had divined the cause. Approximately one thousand years ago the Bonneville landslide had dammed the river, raising the stream's level to the east for nearly twenty miles, and submerging the trees that once stood on the old riverbank. Water-saturated, they were mute testimony to geological events of past eons.

The canyon of the Columbia River was the haunt of interesting creatures. Although the Cascades were formidable obstacles, seals had ascended them. California condors swept from the cliffs and circled on the thermals above the Columbia. "This day we Saw Some fiew of the large Buzzard," wrote Clark. "Capt. Lewis Shot at one, those Buzzards are much larger than any other of ther Spece or the

"Here the mountains leave the river on each Side, which from the great Shute to this place is high and rugid; thickly Covered with timber principally of the Pine Species." William Clark, November 2, 1805

Left: St. Peter's Dome

Above: Wind Mountain (Edward S. Curtis, Oregon Historical Society, Portland, Oregon)

largest Eagle white under part of their wings &c." The Indians possessed the hides of another creature, the mountain goat. "Those animals live among the rocks in those mountains below," noted Clark. The robes made from their pelts had long, coarse hair that, on the back, Clark thought resembled bristles.

West of the Cascades the Corps of Discovery picked up speed and, on November 2, traveled an estimated twenty-nine miles. On the south shore the majestic waterfalls, "Cataracts" on their maps, fell over the cliffs. On November 3 the party was detained for hours by a nearly impenetrable mist that lay over the river and the countryside. The men could not see more than fifty steps, but when the fog lifted, the view was grand. "The Countrey has a handsom appearance," extolled Clark.

Excited by the vistas, Clark set out afoot down the south bank to a river surging out of the hills and into the Columbia. The stream was intriguing. It had a swift current and carried a large volume of water but appeared to be only a few inches deep. "I attempted to wade this Stream and to my astonishment found the bottom a quick Sand, and impassable," he wrote. "I called to the Canoes to put to Shore, I got into the Canoe and landed below the mouth, and Capt. Lewis and my Self walked up this river about 1½ miles to examine this river which we found to be a verry Considerable Stream Dischargeng its waters through 2 Chanels which forms an Island about 3 miles in length on the river and 1½ miles wide." Clark concluded: "This Stream has much the appearance of the *River Platt*: roleing its quick Sands into the bottoms with great velocity."

Lewis and Clark named it the Quicksand River, later known as the Sandy. The party had happened onto an eruptive sequence at Mount Hood in which ash flows poured out of the mountain, melting glaciers and snowfields and sending the muddy mess down the Zigzag and Sandy Rivers. So extensive was this event that the delta of the Sandy, as Clark observed, was "Compressing the waters of the Columbia and throwing the whole Current of its waters against its Northern banks, with a Chanel of ½ a mile wide." A short distance farther downstream the explorers spied Mount Hood, a peak lying southeast nearly forty miles from the mouth of the Quicksand River.

The upper Columbia estuary spread out westward from the Gorge. The river wended its way through large and small islands. While camping on Diamond Island (later known as Government Island), the travelers learned from the Indians that three ships lay in the river below. This was tantalizing news, for, if true, it held the prospect of sending copies of their journals and collections of specimens to President Jefferson by sea. Of equal interest was the improving diet, for the ponds abounded in waterfowl. Clark described a "Sumptious Supper": sandhill crane, wood stork, double-crested cormorant, trumpeter swan, and whistler swan.

The islands were an important winter retreat for the Indians living in the western part of the Columbia Gorge. Their homeland was subject to ice storms, heavy snowfall, and arctic winds. Many of the bands—such as Wah-cle-lahs and Clah-cle-lahs—moved in the winter to the more temperate islands of the upper estuary.

On November 4 the expedition visited a large village on the south shore. Identified as members of the Skil-loot Tribe, a band of Upper Chinookan speakers, the settlement contained twenty-four lodges covered with thatch and bark and one made of split planks, a structure nearly fifty feet long. The village had more than two hundred men and fifty-two canoes pulled up on the bank. Trade goods were readily evident: a sword, guns, powder flasks, jackets, overalls, hats, shirts, beads, and pieces of copper and brass. The residents were friendly and shared with the travelers "roundish roots about the Size of a Small Irish potato." Clark identified this food as *wap-pa-to* and, with Lewis's botanical knowledge, compared it to the arrowhead, a plant cultivated by the Chinese. The plant, *Sagittaria latifolia*, grew in brackish and freshwater ponds along the lower Columbia and in marshy areas of the Willamette Valley. Positive relations soured with the theft of Clark's pipe-tomahawk, and he asserted:

"This remarkable rock which stands on the North shore of the river is unconnected with the hills and rises to the hight of seven hundred feet; it has some pine or reather fir timber on it's northern side, the southern is a precipice of it's whole hight. it rises to a very sharp point and is visible for 20 miles below on the river." Meriwether Lewis, April 6, 1806
Above: Beacon Rock

"Several Sand Islands about noon we halted to dine at the mouth of a River which is filled with quick Sand and is wide and Shallow our officers name this River Quick Sand River on the Lard. Side. here we perceive the tide water." John Ordway, November 3, 1805
Right: Map of Columbia near Quicksand River (Beinecke Library at Yale University)

Overleaf: McCord Creek, Columbia Gorge, Oregon

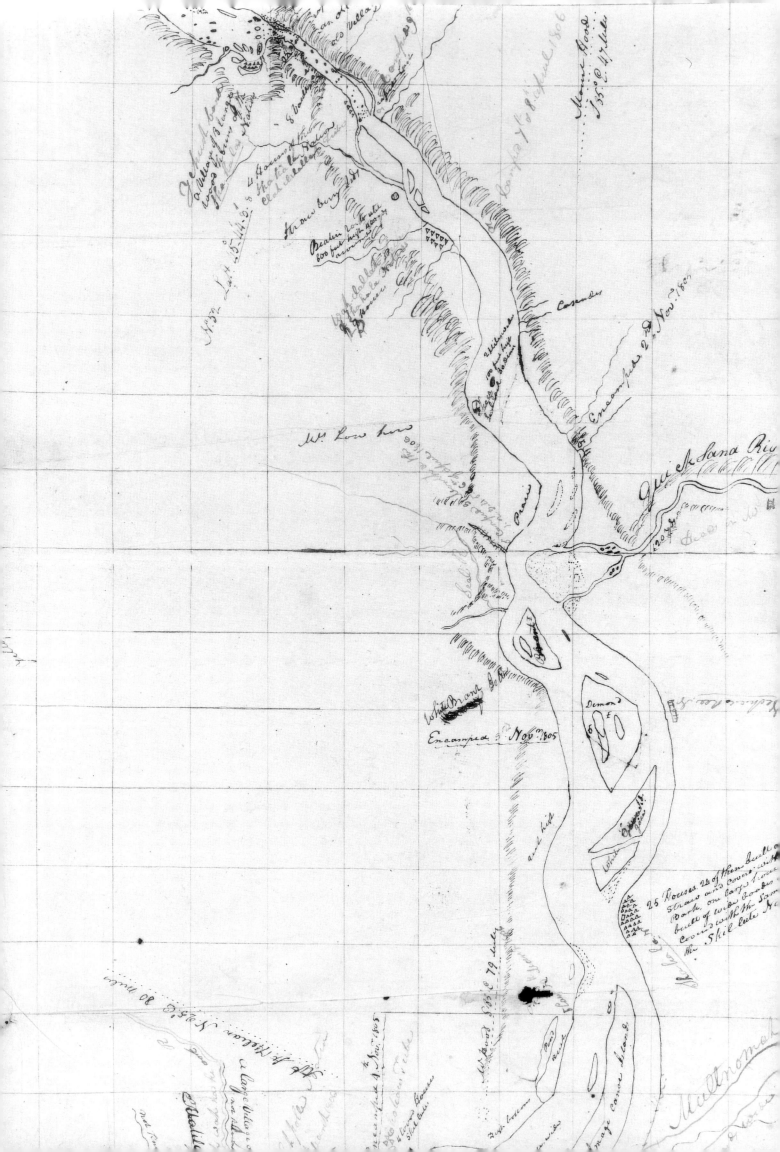

"those fellows we found assumeing and disagreeable, however we Smoked with them and treated them with every attention & friendship."

The explorers missed the mouth of the Willamette in the maze of islands and sloughs. They pressed on, coming into view of Mount Saint Helens, which rose as a nearly perfect snow-covered cone on the northeastern horizon. The party camped amid the sloughs along the river; rain fell. Clark was rueful about the experience: "I [s]lept but verry little last night for the noise Kept dureing the whole of the night by the Swans, Geese, white & Grey Brant Ducks &c. on a Small Sand Island close under the Lard. Side; they were emensely noumerous, and their noise horid." The following day, November 5, the Corps passed Cathlapootle, a large Chinookan village of fourteen lodges at the mouth of the Lewis River. Seven canoes came off to trade. The people, Clark noted, "appeared orderly and well disposed."

November on the Columbia estuary was a bit magical but frustrating. Every day the travelers hoped they might find either a trading ship or the nearby Pacific Ocean. Neither happened. Instead, they paddled steadily with the current and then against the tide, mile after mile. Yellow leaves from the towering cottonwoods floated on the floodtide and mixed with the ochre hues of those falling from the dogwood thickets along the muddy banks. The sedges had turned brown with the chill nights. Lurking in the channels and along the shore were submerged snags, their limbs rippling in the current and threatening to overturn the canoe of the unwary. The hills to the north and south were heavily forested and bathed in fog and mist, except when the deluge of fall rain took control and washed the entire landscape.

The first week of November was cloudy and wet, but steadily the party advanced, tabulating the miles and moving inexorably toward the coast. On November 7 the party camped at Pillar Rock among the Wahkiakum band of Chinooks. Here the men noticed a significant change in the dress of Native women. Rather than tanned hides or modest skirts made of fur, the Wahkiakum women wore fringed hula-like skirts of pounded cedar bark. Soft, pliant, and serviceable, the garments worked much like the fringe on buckskins to draw moisture away from the body.

Then came Grays Bay. At the Marshy Islands the Columbia spread out, broadening to six or eight miles. The waves ran high, surging with the wind against the rocky northern bank of the river where the party followed the primary channel. Some of the men, unaccustomed to the torment of the surf, became seasick, as did Sacagawea. The party put up for the night at Cape Swell, a location on the western margin of Grays Bay, where the surf pounded throughout the night. The Corps spent two nights here, then edged a few more miles along the base of the bluffs.

The following six days and nights were a nightmare. Coasting along the north shore, retreating, advancing, and retreating, the party coped with exposure and extreme frustration. High winds from a southwesterly storm pounded them with gusts and rain, compelling them to move camp, remain, and reconnoiter. The party no longer carried canvas tenting. The men attempted to erect shelters along the narrow beach and maintain blazing fires. Their leather clothing and buffalo robes rotted in the moisture. Winds drove rain sideways into their huts and the tide rose so high with the storm surge that they had to move to higher ground. Lightning flashed, thunder pealed, and hail pelted the wet, miserable campers.

Finally, on November 15, the weather cleared and the party departed in mid-afternoon. The men paddled around Point Ellice, and ahead, on the western horizon, lay the surf of the Pacific. Clark wrote they passed the "blustering point," and beyond found a "butifull Sand beech," a small stream, and a village of thirty-six unoccupied plank houses—the Chinook village of Qwatsa'mts. The structures were filled with fleas. The inhabitants were gone, probably to less exposed camps near the oyster beds on Willapa Bay or hunting sites on nearby rivers. In the lea of a grove of alders, the Corps established its camp. The men appropriated boards from the

"Rained all the last night at intervales of Sometimes of 2 hours. This morning it became Calm & fair. I prepared to Set out at which time the wind sprung up from the S.E. and blew down the River & in a fiew minits raised Such Swells and waves brakeing on the Rocks at the point as to render it unsafe to proceed. I went to the point in an empty canoe and found it would be dangerous to proceed even in an empty Canoe." William Clark, November 15, 1805

Left: Waves pounding on lower Columbia River

Above: Zoomorphic design on basalt hammer (Maryhill Museum, Maryhill, Washington)

Chinook lodges. "Our men all Comfortable," wrote Clark.

Patrick Gass ably summed up the sentiments of the party: "We are now at the end of our voyage, which has been completely accomplished to the intention of the expedition, the object of which was to discover a passage by the way of the Missouri and Columbia rivers to the Pacific ocean; notwithstanding the difficulties, privations and dangers, which we had to encounter, endure and surmount."

Clark, the practical navigator, wasted no words on reflection of a mission accomplished. Instead, he tallied a terse summary:

Ocian 165 miles from *Quick Sand river.*
Ocian 190 Miles from the first rapid.
Ocian 4142 Miles from the Mouth of the *Missouri* R.

Lewis had already pressed on. He was quick to "jump ship" and dash for the prizes of discovery. On November 14, the day before Clark and the main party rounded Point Ellice, Lewis had moved ahead with four men to examine Cape Disappointment, fourteen miles to the west. On November 17, with camp secured, hunters dispatched to try to build up the larder, and Lewis returned from his reconnaissance, Clark set out with ten men who greatly desired to see the ocean from the heights of the headland at the Columbia's mouth. York, Charbonneau, Joseph and Reuben Fields, John Colter, and others made up this detachment; "all others," wrote Clark, "being well Contented with what part of the Ocean & its curiosities which Could be Seen from the vicinity of our Camp."

Clark's exploring party passed through the marshy homeland of the Chinooks, the master makers of canoes and paddles and chief among the trading tribes of the lower Columbia. The explorers, who viewed but the southern border of Chinook territory, estimated their population at four hundred, but did not examine any of their villages on Willapa Bay or its tributaries. Clark, instead, pressed directly to the small bay snug within the eastern face of the cape, to a small island near which the maritime trading ships anchored. "We passed at each point a Soft Clifts of yellow, brown & dark Soft Stones," he wrote, "here Capt. Lewis myself & Severl. of the men marked our names day of the month & by Land &c. &c." "Here I found Capt. Lewis name on a tree," wrote Clark. Fixing names and dates against features at the terminus of their travels gave a finish to the journey. Clark's map included a drawing of a sailing ship in the cove and, on shore, the initials "W.C." and "M.L."

Clark used the highlands at Cape Disappointment to orient the principal features at the mouth of the Columbia. To the east lay Baker Bay, which he identified as "Haley's Bay," named for Haley, a trader who frequently put in to the Columbia to barter with the Chinook Indians. To the south was Point Adams, a low, sandy promontory on the Oregon shore. On the southern horizon loomed the profile of Tillamook Head, a feature Clark identified in his maps as "Clark's Point of View" and so confirmed in the Patrick Gass journal on January 4, 1806. When he hiked along the coast to North Head, Clark gave symmetry to his naming and designated that promontory "Point Lewis." The Indian place names, used from time immemorial, had started on a journey to oblivion. Power lay in the words written in journals and inscribed on maps, and this power belonged to the Corps of Discovery.

During the reconnaissance of the Clark party, Reuben Fields killed a Condor that weighed an estimated twenty-five pounds. The great bird became the object of special interest: "measured from the tips of the wings across 9½ feet, from the point of the Bill to the end of the tail 3 feet 10¼ inches, middle toe 5½ inches, toe nale 1 inch & 3½ lines, wing feathers 2½ feet long and 1 inch 5 lines diamiter tale feathers 14½ inches, and the *head* is 6½ inches including the beak." Jefferson had wanted precise observations. The journals recorded details. The head of the condor went into a carrying case and, ultimately, became an exhibit in the museum of Charles Wilson Peale in Baltimore and Philadelphia.

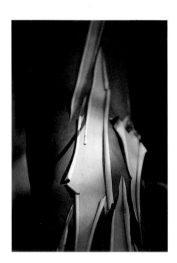

"The tree which bears a red burry in clusters of a round form and size of a red haw. the leaf like that of the small magnolia, and brark smoth and of a brickdust red coulour it appears to be of the evergreen kind." Meriwether Lewis, December 1, 1805
*Above: Madrone
(Arbutus menziesii) tree bark*

"The Sea which is imedeately in front roars like a repeeted roling thunder and have rored in that way ever Since our arrival in its borders which is now 24 Days Since we arrived in Sight of the Great Western Ocian, I cant Say Pasific as Since I have Seen it, it has been the reverse." William Clark, December 1, 1805
*Right: Pacific Ocean
north of Tillamook Head*

The dealings of the Chinooks with Americans and Europeans had begun in 1792, when Captain Robert Gray of Boston and Lieutenant William R. Broughton of England sailed over the bar and entered the Columbia estuary. Experienced by centuries of pre-contact trade, the Chinooks knew how to drive hard bargains. Their tenacity and haggling dumbfounded the members of the Corps of Discovery. The Lewis and Clark Expedition was at a great disadvantage. Their trade goods were meager, confined to a slender inventory carried across the continent, rather than the mass of articles stowed in the hull of a sailing ship. To their dismay they discovered that the number one items of favor with the Chinooks were blue beads—dark cobalt pieces of glass. Their inventory contained mostly common white beads, and there were none too many of those.

On November 20, Clark returned to the base camp at Qwatsa'mts, encountering along the way several groups of Chinooks. They gave Clark dried sturgeon and wapato and agreed, for the payment of a fishhook, to paddle one of the canoes to camp. Clark walked along the beach and found many of the tribe, including Chiefs Com-com-mo-ly and Chil-lar-la-wil, visiting Lewis and the others. One of the chiefs wore a robe of stunning sea otter pelts. "Both Capt. Lewis & my Self endeavored to purchase the *roab* with differant articles," wrote Clark. "At length we precured it for a belt of blue beeds which the Squar—wife of our interpreter Shabono wore around her waste." Sacagawea appeared remarkably compliant, perhaps because the captains had chastised her husband when he beat her.

Four days later, Sacagawea participated in an unusual event for a military expedition. Lewis and Clark asked all in the party—including York and the Indian woman—to participate in a poll indicating where they wished to spend the winter. The options—tallied in cryptic shorthand in Clark's journal—were probably the south shore of the Columbia, the mouth of the Sandy River, the "Friendly Village" below Celilo Falls and the Narrows, and "Lookout" and "up," presumably points somewhere east along the Columbia River. The only person failing to indicate a preference was the errant Charbonneau. Clark, however, wrote: "Solicitations of every individual, except one of our party induced us Conclude to Cross the river and examine the opposit Side." The preferences tallied twenty-seven for crossing to the south shore, one against; if the setting proved unsuitable, then there was a tally of six for the "falls," ten for "Sandy River," and twelve for "lookout up."

Captain Lewis made clear his interest in the south shore of the Columbia. He argued that if hunting proved promising, the site would also give the men an opportunity to try to boil salt out of seawater. If not, he was willing to move east to the Sandy River. Captain Clark wanted to examine the south shore to assess the disposition of the Clatsops and ascertain the prospects of a vessel putting into the river. He argued that encountering a trading ship and securing goods for the nearly naked men would more than offset subsisting on poor elk and deer in the region. Clark, added, however, that if those prospects were not realized, he favored going as far east as the "Friendly Village." "Salt water I view as an evil in as much as it is not helthy," he warned.

The reasons for exploring the south shore were compelling. It was less exposed than the windswept north bank. Clatsop Indians, visiting the base camp near Point Ellice, had reported an abundance of elk, a creature easier to hunt in winter and whose hides made good clothing. The Chinooks were sharp traders and demanded such high prices that the Corps would soon run out of beads, ribbons, and other items if it had to continue bartering for food. A south shore site might also facilitate meeting a sailing ship, as well as provide ease of access to the beach where the men could boil seawater to extract salt. Cogent arguments thus led to the note penned on November 25 by Joseph Whitehouse: "Our Officers had concluded on crossing the River, & endeavor to find out a suitable place for our Winter Quarters."

The Corps of Discovery broke camp and returned along the north shore to a point where the captains concluded they might cross the Columbia with reasonable

"Great numbers of Swan Geese Brant Ducks & Gulls in this great bend which is Crouded with low Islands covered with weeds grass &c. and overflowed every flood tide." William Clark, November 16, 1805

Left: Islands and channels, lower Columbia in the Lewis & Clark National Wildlife Refuge, Oregon

safety. The men paddled for nine miles, then turned into the currents and tides. Waves threatened to engulf and sink their canoes. Abandoning the effort, they returned to the bank and continued east another four miles and camped near Pillar Rock. The Corps here found a considerably shorter transit and the shelter of several islands, through which they wended their way to the south bank.

The captains established a base camp on the narrow peninsula attaching Tongue Point to the mainland. For ten days—November 27 to December 7—the party camped at this site. Rains hammered them. The winds tore at their rude shelters so furiously that the men thought the trees in the forest would be uprooted. "Those Squals were Suckceeded by rain," wrote Clark. "!O how Tremendious is the day." Held down by the winds and unable to proceed in the dugouts, the men scoured the countryside for game and attempted to mend their tattered leather outfits.

Lewis and a patrol of five set out on November 29 to explore the prospects for a winter encampment. During his absence, Clark wrote brief notes about snails, worms, spiders, flies, lizards, and other creatures. Sacagawea, clearly a woman who appreciated Captain Clark's leadership and intercession on her behalf with her hapless husband, presented him a piece of bread made of flour. She had reserved this morsel for her infant son, but it had gotten wet and a little sour in the rainy camp, and she felt she had to use it. "This bread I eate with great Satisfaction, it being the only mouthfull I had tasted for Several months past," Clark wrote.

Boredom, gastrointestinal problems, hunger, weeping eyes tormented by smoke, and general misery beset the men. "O! how disagreeable my Situation," lamented Clark on December 3. The wind continued to blow. The diet consisted of a few elk marrow bones, wapato roots, pounded fish, and sometimes a bit of elk soup. The idle hours gave Clark time to leave more evidence of his presence. On a large pine tree on the peninsula he carved: "Capt William Clark December 3rd 1805. By Land. U States in 1804 & 1805." Sacagawea helped prepare his meals. "After eateing the marrow out of two Shank bones of an Elk," wrote Clark, "the Squar choped the bones fine boiled them and extraacted a pint of Grease, which is Superior to the tallow of the animal."

"Capt Lewis's long delay below," wrote Clark on December 5, "has been the cause of no little uneasiness on my part for him, a 1000 conjectures has crouded into my mind respecting his probable Situation & Safty." But just when the concern was highest, Lewis and three men returned. Lewis reported the countryside rugged and its forests almost impenetrable, but he had found a suitable site for a camp on a small river on the south side of the great estuary. Lewis's men had shot six elk and five deer during their travels. "This was verry Satisfactory information to all the party," wrote Clark. "We accordingly deturmined to proceed on to the Situation which Capt. Lewis had Viewed as Soon as the wind and weather Should permit and Comence building huts &c."

On December 7 the Corps of Discovery began moving once again. Clark wrote:

we assended a river which falls in on the South Side of this Bay 3 miles to the first point of high land on the West Side, the place Capt. Lewis had viewed and formed in a thick groth of pine about 200 yards from the river, this situation is on a rise about 30 feet higher than the high tides leavel and thickly Covered with lofty pine. This is certainly the most eligable Situation for our purposes of any in its neighborhood.

The tasks ahead were daunting. The captains ordered the men to fell trees, first to create a clearing in the forest and second to cut logs into manageable lengths, carry them to the site, and erect their huts. As at Fort Mandan on the banks of the Missouri the previous year, the captains designed a defensible outpost. The men laid foundation logs on December 10 and moved swiftly, inspired by the unrelenting rain. Four days later, Patrick Gass wrote: "We completed the building of our huts, 7 in number, all but the covering, which I now find will not be so difficult as I expected; as we have found

"The roots are of a superior quality to any I had before seen: they are called whapto; resemble a potato when cooked, and are about as big as a hen egg." Patrick Gass, November 4, 1805

Right: Edible roots of the wapato (Sagittaria latifolia)

a kind of timber in plenty, which splits freely and makes the finest puncheons I have ever seen." While the men may have split fir boards, it is likely they used cedar for roofing planks. Several also went by canoe to an abandoned Clatsop village and appropriated planks, undoubtedly cedar. Finish work, including chinking the walls and constructing chimneys, continued for several days.

Fort Clatsop was nearly square and consisted of two sets of huts facing each other with a small, interior parade ground, both ends enclosed with a stockade. Clark's elkskin-bound journal contained two floor plans of the structure. Three rooms for the men stood along the west side; four rooms, including bunking space for the captains, a meat room for smoking game, a place for the Charbonneau family, and a workroom with fireplace on its west wall were on the east side. Undoubtedly the fort was muddy, riven with roots, interrupted with stumps, and littered with chips from the nearly ceaseless chopping during the several days of construction. When the gates closed at night, the little outpost was a quiet but firm intrusion into the Indian domain of the vast Columbia watershed. Its inhabitants were the advance guard of the changes afoot in the land.

Construction of the fort exacted a toll. The men suffered from boils, a displaced shoulder, dysentery, and a strained knee. All were beset with fleas that lurked in their buckskin outfits and buffalo robes and blankets. Many days the crew was hungry. Respite appeared more certain when, on December 13, George Drouillard and George Shannon killed eighteen elk, sixteen of which they found and butchered. Two days later the captains dispatched sixteen men with three canoes to retrieve these vital supplies.

On Christmas day 1805, Gass noted: "This morning we left our camp and moved into our huts. At daybreak all the men paraded and fired a round of small arms, wishing the commanding officers a merry Christmas." Clark and Lewis distributed a portion of the scarce remaining store of tobacco to those who used it; to others, they gave hand-kerchiefs. "We had no ardent spirit of any kind among us," wrote Joseph Whitehouse, "but are mostly in good health, A blessing, which we esteem more, than all the luxuries this life can afford, and the party are all thankful to the Supreme Being, for his good-ness towards us."

Clark noted that he received several presents: a pair of moccasins from Whitehouse, two dozen weasel tails from Sacagawea, and a shirt, drawers, and a pair of stockings from Lewis. "We would have Spent this day the nativity of Christ in feasting," wrote Clark, "had we any thing either to raise our Sperits or even gratify our appetites." Christmas dinner at Fort Clatsop, 1805, was a meal of poor elk, "So much Spoiled," lamented Clark, "that we eate it thro' mear necessity." The men supplemented the meal with spoiled, pounded fish, and roots.

As darkness swept over the new military outpost in the forest on the south bank of the Columbia River, the Corps of Discovery settled in for the winter. The men had braved the treacherous waters of the great river of the west in their fragile dugout canoes, portaged the Cascades, explored the vast estuary, surmounted the heights of Cape Disappointment, and found a suitable place to spend the winter. Without rain-proof clothing, tenting, flashlights, matches, gas stoves, or repeating rifles, they had coped remarkably well. The tasks of the next dozen weeks were clear: stay on good terms with the nearby Clatsop Indians, manufacture salt, kill and carry game to camp, make leather clothing for the return journey, and keep a close watch for any ship entering the river.

The assignments for the two captains were equally demanding. The sojourn at Fort Clatsop gave them time to come to terms with Jefferson's assignments. As at Fort Mandan, they now had residency in one place and the leisure to prepare maps, observe and note the lifeways of the Indians, record vocabularies, write expansive journal entries, and where possible, secure scientific specimens. Above all, they needed to maintain discipline and morale among the men, doctoring them for their ailments, keeping them engaged in work, and preparing for the long journey home.

"I am informed that the *Chinnook* Nation inhabit this low countrey and live in large wood houses on a river which passes through this bottom Parrilal to the Sea coast and falls into the Bay" William Clark, November 19, 1805

Left: Island in Willapa Bay

"Mount Hood appears near the River on the South Side which is covd. thick with Snow & very white."

John Ordway, April 14, 1806

Above: Mount Hood, Oregon

Here the river widens to near a mile, and the bottoms are more extensive and thickly timbered, as also the high mountains on each Side, with Pine, Spruce pine, Cotton wood, a species of ash, and alder. William Clark, November 2, 1805

Right: Black cottonwood leaves (Populus trichocarpa). *Observed on the Columbia River, 1806*

"We saw some turkey buzzards this morning
of the species common to the United states which
are the first we have seen on this side
of the rocky mountains."

Meriwether Lewis, Columbia Gorge, April 9, 1806

Above: Turkey vulture (Cathartes aura)

A cloudy foggey morning Some rain. we Set out early proceeded under the Stard Shore
under a high rugid hills with Steep assent the Shore boalt and rockey, the fog So thick
we could not See across the river. William Clark, November 7, 1805

Left: Falls on a tributary to the Columbia at Stella, Washington

Winter at Fort Clatsop, 1805–6

"I took a run the other day up the Lewis & Clark's river as it is called to the place of the W[inter] encampment, which long as I have been here I never visited before. The site of their log hut is still visible, the foundation logs rotting where they lay. Their old trail to the coast is just visible being much overgrown with brush. Their camp was about 4 miles from the beach."

George Gibbs, Astoria, Oregon, April 13, 1853

Winters on the Northwest Coast can be cruel and numbing in their monotony and torment of ceaseless gray days and rain. The winter of 1805–6 gave no slack to the Corps of Discovery. It rolled in with southwesterly storms and continued to assault the shoreline day after day, week after week, choking the streams with its deluge. Conditions were great for ducks, geese, fleas, slugs, and moss, but miserable for a small company of military men, a woman, and a child trying to endure until they could turn around and head home across the continent.

January 1, 1806, the men of the expedition saluted the day by firing a volley of small arms outside the room of Captains Lewis and Clark, and presented their leaders with tasty morsels—to each a fresh elk tongue and marrow bones for a New Year's feast. Lewis, often reflective and renewing his commitment to write a journal after a hiatus of months, thought about where he might be a year hence. He wrote that the day "consisted principally in the anticipation of the 1st day of January 1807, when in the bosom of our friends we hope to participate in the mirth and hilarity of the day, and when with the zest given by the recollection of the present, we shall completely, both mentally and corporally, enjoy the repast which the hand of civilization has prepared for us." Eating boiled elk and wapato and toasting the new year with water clearly caused Lewis to focus on the renewal of fellowship in "civilized society."

The captains instituted a new military regimen for the post. They were concerned about the coming and going of local Indians, the prospect of theft of valued tools or weapons, and the security of their station. The numbers of personnel at the fort varied because of the arrival and departure of hunting parties, the manning of the saltworks camp on the coast, and exploring missions around the mouth of the river. Henceforth, Fort Clatsop was to have a twenty-four-hour guard: a sergeant and three privates, with one, a sentinel, on duty day and night. While all Indians were to be treated in a "friendly manner," they were to be escorted from the fort at sundown when the guard would close the main gate and staff the "water gate" closer to the river.

Lewis and Clark laid down other rules. The men were to check the canoes at least once every twenty-four hours, deliver two loads of firewood to the captains' quarters each morning, maintain perpetual fires in the smokehouse, and return immediately any metal tool used for any purpose once the task was completed. Should theft occur, they mandated immediate reporting of the incident. The captains announced the rules and recorded no complaints. The worst situation was the continuing assault of fleas. Lewis referred to them as the "intolerable vermin," while Clark lamented the bites of "those disagreeable insects."

The new year brought a visit from Chief Co-mo-wool (or Coboway) of the Clatsops, who came to trade roots, dogs, and fresh blubber for manufactured goods. In spite of ardent hunting for elk, the men were famished and responded hungrily to the report that a whale had washed ashore in the territory of the Tillamooks to the south. "This blubber the Indians eat and esteeme it excellent food," wrote Lewis. He noted that since embarking on a diet of dog meat along the Clearwater, Snake, and Columbia, the exploring party had become "much more healthy strong and more fleshy." Lewis was often hungry, a subject confirmed by such lines in his diary as: "for

"We completed the building of our huts, 7 in number, all but the covering, which I now find will not be so difficult as I expected; as we have found a kind of timber in plenty, which splits freely, and makes the finest puncheons I have ever seen. They can be split 10 feet long and two broad, not more than an inch and an half thick." Patrick Gass, September 14, 1805

Left: Fort Clatsop, National Historic Monument, Warrenton, Oregon

my own part I have become so perfectly reconciled to the dog that I think it an agreeable food and would prefer it vastly to lean Venison or Elk." He added further: "I get fat meat, for as to species of meat I am not very particular, the flesh of the dog the horse and the wolf, having from habit become equally formiliar with any other, and I have learned to think that if the chord be sufficiently strong, which binds the soul and boddy together, it dose not so much matter about the materials which compose it."

Clark thought otherwise, generally despising dog meat, wolf, crow, and other game which sometimes fell into the Corps's cooking pots. He perceived the grounding of a whale as an ideal opportunity to try to obtain a large supply of meat for the party. Such an undertaking would also permit him to check on the saltworks and mount a reconnaissance south along the coast comparable to that which he had run north from Cape Disappointment. On January 6, Clark departed from Fort Clatsop with twelve men, the Charbonneau family, and two canoes. Sacagawea had given him an ultimatum about going. "She observed that She had traveled a long way with us to See the great waters, and that now that monstrous fish was also to be Seen, She thought it verry hard that She Could not be permitted to See either." Clark relented.

Clark hired a Tillamook guide at the saltmakers' camp, paying him a file and promising additional goods at the completion of the mission. At the north margin of Tillamook Head, the guide pointed and said, *"Pe Shack"* ("bad" or "dangerous"). Then commenced the arduous ascent, nearly fifteen hundred feet straight up by difficult trail on which travelers, in places, had to pull themselves along by grabbing roots and shrubs. The muddy, upward route required two hours of climbing. "From the top . . . I looked down with estonishment," wrote Clark, "to behold the hight which we had asended." At this moment he turned to see fourteen Indians, men and women, loaded down with blubber and oil and about to descend to the beach below.

The patrol camped on the headland. Part of the area was heavily forested, for Clark later remarked that some of the trees towered as much as 210 feet high and were 8 to 12 feet in diameter. In 1806 a portion of Tillamook Head—identified in the expedition maps and journals as Clark's Point of View—was open ground. At several places along the coast of present-day Oregon, especially where villages stood at the base of south-facing slopes, the Indians burned the headlands for security, removing trees and brush and lessening the prospect of surprise attack by enemies. Clark wrote: "at 1½ miles arived at a Open where I had a view of the Seas Coast for a long Distance rocks in every direction."

The party proceeded south, crossing three rugged promontories jutting into the sea, and arrived at the mouth of a creek where it found the butchered remains of a great whale lying on the sand. The scene was lively. Some of the Tillamooks were busily boiling whale oil in a twenty-foot-long trough by dropping in heated stones. They stored the rendered oil in bladders and part of the whale intestines. For the villagers at Ecola, the "place of the whale," the event was perhaps a once-in-a lifetime opportunity to draw visitors and payments for the bounty washed ashore.

Clark managed to purchase a few gallons of oil and approximately three hundred pounds of blubber, all he could afford but certainly not the amount he desired. Nevertheless, the American military leader was happy: "Small as this Stock is," he wrote, "I prise it highly; and thank providence for directing the whale to us; and think him much more kind to us than he was to jonah, having Sent this monster to be *Swallowed by us* in Sted of *Swallowing of us* as jonah's did." The encounter at Ecola also permitted Clark to secure information on the Tillamook Indians. Based on the rudimentary information, he sketched a map showing "Calamox" (Tillamook) Bay, five primary tributaries draining into it, a total of forty plank houses, and four primary, named villages.

Clark and his party turned around on January 9 to return to Fort Clatsop. He divided up the whale items—blubber, jaw and rib bones, and oil—for all to carry and

To-mar-lar from Grand chief

Wal lar war lar,

Yel lep pit Chief

made a Chief any and a
double chief
cart and seal by name of
Ar-lo-qual ———— of the
sioux
sioux Nation ————

Presented to I. I. Audubon
at St Louis April 19th 1843 –
by D. D. Mitchell Supt.
Indian Affairs.

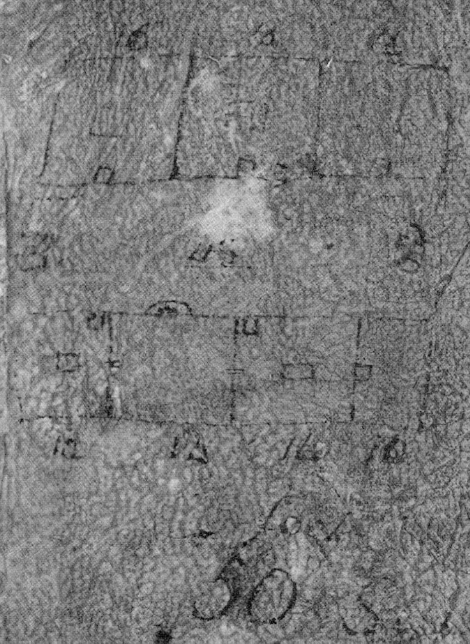

set out shortly after sunrise to retrace their steps over Tillamook Head. They spent the night, quite exhausted, at the saltmakers' camp, and returned to Fort Clatsop the following day.

The crew remaining at Fort Clatsop was not idle during the absence of the whale patrol. Lewis wrote that the men were hunting, smoking meat, and sewing clothing of elk and deer hides. Their winter assignment was to manufacture dozens of pairs of moccasins and leather pants and shirts for the return journey. Lewis wrote briefly on burial practices of the local tribes and entertained a visiting Cathlamet chief and his retinue. They brought mats, dogs, wapato, and dried salmon and expected good payment; Lewis had little to offer.

Mid-January was not a good time for hunting, nor for the expedition's canoes. On January 11, the prized "Indian canoe," one sufficiently light that four men could readily portage it a mile, vanished. It had played important service in carrying more than one thousand pounds of freight and up to three passengers. Search parties found no trace of it. Only four days later one of the large dugouts disappeared. Its tie-up rope had separated; fortunately a detachment found and retrieved it. The captains then laid down tighter rules for management of the vessels: three were to be pulled ashore, above the reach of currents and tides; and a fourth canoe was to be moored in the inlet upstream from the landing where it would not get washed away.

Spirits soared on January 12 when George Drouillard, the finest marksman in the party, felled seven elk. The captains ordered it all to be jerked and rationed out as needed. The men retrieved the elk. They also began to render out tallow and added a new task to their daily assignment—candle making. Camp labors now included carrying, butchering, and jerking elk meat; cutting and sewing clothing; and making candles, cooking, and rotating guard duty. "We have plenty of Elk beef for the present and a little salt," wrote Lewis. "Our houses dry and comfortable, and having made up our minds to remain until the 1st of April, every one appears content with his situation and his fare."

January labors for Meriwether Lewis were primarily ethnographic. Each day he took on a new subject. He began with Clatsop and Chinook hunting practices and described their use of muskets, bows and arrows, snares, spears, and dead fall traps. He admired their handsome, sinew-backed bows and the composite arrows that, when shot into a lake or river, permitted the recovery of at least the feathered portion of the main shaft. He noted that tips of stone, copper, and iron were nearly equal in use, and that their muskets, obtained through trade, were often in poor repair because they were damaged by the use of stones for projectiles.

Lewis next turned to fishing. The Clatsop and Chinooks, he reported, used hooks and lines, gigs, scooping or dipnets with long handles, and large seine nets. The "straight" or seine net they used in the estuary to encircle schools of migrating fish. Lewis then shifted his writing to culinary objects by assessing the wooden bowls, baskets, spoons, serving mats, and cooking spits that made up the kitchen inventory in the Indian lodges. He admired greatly the wooden bowls and the troughs for boiling fish and rendering oil, describing them as "extremely well executed" and "neatly carved." He described their method of baking salmon: filleting the fish, impaling it on a split cedar spit, inserting narrow splints to keep the flesh together, and cooking it head-down by leaning the fillet toward the fire.

The quality of Lewis's observations was confirmed daily. When he switched to housing, he provided measurements and details of construction so accurate that two centuries later it would be possible to replicate a Clatsop lodge solely on the basis of the word pictures he penned. He noted the size of the smoke hole in the cedar plank ceiling, use of withes to bind planks to the framing, notching of the major house supports to hold the roof beams, size of the semi-subterranean hearth and activity area, construction of beds and shelving around the outer walls, and hanging of racks in

"The waves appear to brake with tremendious force in every direction quite across a large Sand bar lies within the mouth nearest to point Adams which is nearly covered at high tide." William Clark, November 18, 1805

Left: Pacific Ocean looking toward Tillamook Head from the mouth of the Columbia River

the ceiling for smoking fish and meat. In an era decades before the emergence of ethnography as a discipline, Meriwether Lewis was engaged in defining it by his cogent observations.

The sleek and seaworthy canoes of the Chinookans at the mouth of the Columbia fascinated the Corps of Discovery. Their awkward pine dugouts that had carried them downstream from the mouth of the North Fork of the Clearwater inspired them to covet the craft of the Indians at the mouth of the Columbia. "I have seen the natives near the coast riding waves in these canoes," wrote Lewis, "with safety and apparently without concern where I should have thought it impossible for any vessel of the same size to lived a minute." The sleek craft had high, flaring gunwales to keep out water and were carved almost paper-thin from single cedar logs.

Some Chinook and Clatsop canoes were fifty feet long and could carry as much as ten thousand pounds of cargo or twenty to thirty persons. Each was custom designed with effigies on the bow and stern. These sculptural figures rose as high as five feet and were attached to the craft with wooden dowels or pegs. "When the natives are engaged in navigating their canoes," wrote Lewis, "one sets in the stern and steers with a paddle the others set by pears and paddle over the gunwall next to them, they all kneel in the bottom of the canoe and set on their feet." The prowess of the Chinooks and Clatsops in commerce was directly related to their skill in manufacturing and operating their magnificent canoes.

Lewis also wrote about family relations, multigenerational households, treatment of the elderly, and the tenuous nature of leadership among the Chinookans. He was afforded ample opportunity to make these observations by the steady flow of visitors to the fort, as well as his sojourns to villages, where he had the chance to enter the lodges and see, as best he could, the dynamics of everyday life.

Although the flowering plants were dormant and the hardwood trees and shrubs had lost their leaves, in late January Lewis began recording botanical observations. Similar to his approach in compiling ethnographic data, Lewis usually took on one subject each day. His time spent with Dr. Benjamin Smith Barton in Philadelphia resounded in what he wrote. Barton, author of *Elements of Botany* (1803), introduced Lewis to the rudiments of analysis, identification, and description of plants. The impact of the crash course, as well as his use of Barton's book (part of the expedition's traveling library) and the taxonomy of Linnaeus, were confirmed in his journals.

On January 21, Lewis described the thistle, called *Shan-ne-tah-que* by the Clatsops who dug and roasted its edible roots. Lewis described it with an impressive vocabulary of technical terms: fusiform, radicles, cauline leaf, crenate, hairy, decurrent, declining, and pericap. In his plant descriptions he discussed everything from root to seeds, color to condition of leaves and stems. In spite of the rigors of travel by water, the horribly wet weather of the seacoast, and field conditions generally, Lewis collected, pressed, preserved, and brought to the East Coast 239 specimens of 177 different species. Lewis was the pioneering botanist in the upper Missouri and Columbia watersheds and left a fascinating legacy, for many of his commentaries included Indian plant names, medicinal and food uses, and comments upon the impact of weather and other conditions on the growth and distribution of plants.

When Lewis identified and described the bracken fern—a plant with wide distribution around the northern hemisphere—he crafted an essay of nearly four hundred words. He worked under adverse circumstances because, as he noted, the plant was "of course dead at present." Lewis probably brought each specimen to his quarters and, sitting by the open fire with the flickering of a candle, painstakingly examined the plant and penned his observations. As the winter days passed, Lewis worked his way through the flora growing in the vicinity of Fort Clatsop. Each time he considered a new specimen, he described it in as much detail as he could muster. He expressed awe at the tremendous Sitka spruce that hugged the fog-shrouded

coastline at the mouth of the Columbia. He measured and reported their maximum circumference to be as much as 30 feet, while he estimated their maximum height at 230 feet. He described the needles as acerose, acuminate, and sessile. A practical man, he also observed that the spruce "rives" or splits "better than any other species which we have tryed."

Food remained a concern. The men consumed the salt from the camp at the mouth of the Necanicum River almost as fast as it was obtained. Clark voiced anxiety about the vanishing foodstuffs. He wrote that on January 18 he and Lewis had issued a ration of six pounds of jerked elk meat per man but that in two and a half days it was all gone. "At this rate our Seven Elk will only last us 3 days longer," he lamented, "yet no one appears much concerned about the State of the Stores." Clark concluded that the skill of the hunters was the greatest consolation, for if any game could be found, they usually bagged it.

The hunting parties were sometimes absent from the fort or saltworks camp for days, and the rain fell almost without interruption. The forest understory was dank, wet, swampy, cold, and confusing. Many of the large trees had toppled over in wind storms, which left gaping holes and towering mounds of roots obstructing both the view and easy progress. At night the hunters hunkered down under a robe of damp elkskins or their blankets, shivering around a fire with one side too warm and the other damp and cold, trying to sleep and regain their energy for another day of pursuing elk or hefting carcasses to the fort. John Ordway, writing while on a patrol to the saltworks, described the conditions: "much fatigued and I am at this time verry Sick, and wet to my Skins waiding the Slashes and marshes. the day verry disagreeable and Stormey."

The hunting prowess of George Drouillard and others greatly impressed the Clatsops. Often when the men were butchering elk, they found projectiles that the Indians had shot but that had not killed these large animals. The rifles of the Corps were more powerful than the bows and arrows and old muskets of the Indian hunters. Lewis also demonstrated the experimental air gun that he had used throughout the journey. "My Air-gun also astonishes them very much," he wrote, "they cannot comprehend it's shooting so often and without powder; and think that it is *great medicine* which comprehends every thing that is to them incomprehensible."

The appetites of the Corps of Discovery were not only for food. Sex was also on the agenda, but such adventures with the Indian women proved dangerous to health. Thirteen years of contact with shiploads of maritime traders had fostered a commerce in prostitution. The first encounter with this "traffic" occurred when camping among the Chinooks. On November 21, 1805, Clark wrote: "Several Indians and Squars came this evening I beleave for the purpose of gratifying the passions of our men." Two months later Lewis wrote: "Goodrich has recovered from the Louis veneri [*Loues venerea*] which he contracted from an amorous encounter with a Chinnook damsel. I cured him as I did Gibson last winter by the uce of murcury." The ravages of venereal disease were evident among the Native population, and in skin lesions and pustules affecting the health and appearance of the men in the expedition. The treatment with mercury, part of the regimen of Dr. Benjamin Rush of Philadelphia, reduced the symptoms, but amounted to treating the ailment with poison, negatively affecting the health of those so doctored.

Throughout their travels, the two captains appear to have abstained from sexual relations with the Indian women. When the occasion arose, they turned down the opportunity. Their behavior was probably one of leading by example, setting themselves apart from the men in the Corps and, without acknowledgment as such, maintaining a protocol of aloof and formal relations with the tribes. Throughout his writings, Lewis evidenced great awkwardness and, at times, prudery in describing the naked or nearly naked bodies of Indian women. His comments suggest either an incomplete definition of his sexuality or a nearly pathological shyness in the company of women.

"(No. 1.) a species which grows to immence size; very commonly 27 feet in the girth six feet above the surface of the earth, and in several instances we have found them as much as 36 feet in the girth or 12 feet diameter perfectly solid and entire. they frequently rise to the hight of 230 feet, and one hundred and twenty or 30 of that hight without a limb. this timber is white and soft throughout and rives better than any other species which we have tryed. the bark skales off in irregula rounded flakes and is of a redish brown colour particularly of the younger growth." Meriwether Lewis, February 4, 1806

Left: Sitka spruce (Picea sitchensis). Observed September 16, 1805, Lolo Trail.

The care of the men was as important as attention to the slender stock of critical supplies. While the trade items diminished steadily through the purchase of foodstuffs, guide service, and diplomatic relations, the critical firepower of the party was also of concern. On February 1 the captains ordered the men to open all of the lead canisters carrying powder and ball. A total of forty canisters remained in the inventory, and from the contents of these the Corps had to sustain and protect itself for the rest of the winter and during the return journey. Each canister contained four pounds of powder and eight pounds of lead. Thirty-five canisters were in perfect condition; five were damaged with some loss of firepower. Prudence had dictated the policy of distributing the canisters among the canoes. Clark asserted that the contents of the canisters were the "only hope for Subsistance and defences in the rout of 4,000 miles through a Country exclusively inhabited by Indians—many bands of which are Savage in every Sense of the word." The assessment of the inventory confirmed that the Corps was sufficiently outfitted with powder and lead to hunt and defend itself, if it embraced stewardship and care.

By mid-February the captains optimistically concluded that they had enough jerked and smoked elk meat to sustain the party to the end of their sojourn at the fort. Their concern for the health of the men was constant; "we are very uneasy with rispect to our sick men at the salt works," wrote Lewis on February 14. The site was exposed to the constant buffeting of the southwesterly storms. The men were besieged by chill blasts of winds and were almost constantly wet, either from going into the surf to fill their kettles with saltwater or from pursuing elk in the nearby forest. The captains, at one point, sent not only relief men to replace those at the saltworks but also a detachment to carry George Gibson in a litter to Fort Clatsop. Suffering from a fever and "much reduced" in health, Gibson had contracted a cold and became increasingly ill. Lewis and Clark dosed him with potassium nitrate, sage tea, and laudanum (opium), bathing his feet in warm water and inducing both sweating and sleep. When Gibson did not immediately recover, they treated him with the elixir of health—"Dr. Rushes pills." Either the treatments or nature took its course, for Gibson recovered.

During the wintry days of January and February, Clark pored over the sketch maps and latitude and longitude that he and Lewis had dutifully recorded throughout their travels. On February 14 Lewis reported that three days before, "Capt. Clark completed a map of the country through which we have been passing from Fort Mandan to this place." In a lengthy journal entry, Lewis wrestled with the geography of the upper Missouri. He realized that by following the river's course to its headwaters, the expedition had followed Jefferson's instructions but had not found the shortest and best route. Reflecting on what was known, Lewis boldly asserted: "we now discover that we have found the most practicable and navigable passage across the Continent of North America." That passage, deduced from the information on Clark's map and input from Indians, convinced the captains that a shortcut from the Bitterroot Valley via the Clark Fork of the Columbia to the Great Falls would cut dozens and dozens of miles off the route.

The cartographic labors helped fix in the minds of the captains strategies for examining terrain during the return journey. Most importantly, Clark's map dramatically filled in the void of geographical knowledge about a vast section of the American West. The map he prepared in the firelight of the captains' quarters represented a monumental advance in coming to terms with "terra incognita," the words that heretofore had held dominion over the hinterlands of the western part of the continent.

As February drifted by in drizzling days and nights, Meriwether Lewis sustained his prolific production of journal entries on the flora and fauna of the American West. While he concentrated on local specimens, his comments often included area distribution of plants and animals and, at times, comparisons with their relatives on

"The Crow raven and Large Blackbird are the same as those of our country only that the crow is here much smaller yet it's note is the same." Meriwether Lewis, March 3, 1806
Right: Raven
(Corvus corax sinuatus)

the other side of the continent. Lewis wrote an admiring commentary on the sea otter, described the harbor seal, assessed the features of the raccoon, and described the small, brown squirrel. A white-tailed rabbit that came into his hands before it headed to a cooking pot elicited a fulsome description, including measurements of its ears, tail, body, and feet.

The journals reveal that Lewis painstakingly measured his specimens. Perhaps his steely concentration on the size of things was a legacy of Jefferson's debate with Comte Georges de Buffon, the French physician and botanist who had argued that degeneracy marked the mammals of North America. According to the theory, climate and hostile conditions in the New World doomed man and beast to mental, moral, and physical inferiority. Jefferson contested the hypothesis and insisted that North American mammals were consistently larger than those in Europe. Similarly he asserted that Native Americans had demonstrated remarkably robust health, mental prowess, and eloquence. "It is one of those cases where judgment has been seduced by a glowing pen," wrote Jefferson. So at Fort Clatsop, the pen of Captain Lewis recorded the data and added more ammunition to the President's long-waged assertion that Buffon and his associates were simply wrong about the Western Hemisphere.

When local Indians brought eulachon or smelt to the fort, Lewis became an admiring artist. The eulachon was a seasonal visitor to the Columbia estuary and its upriver reaches. Its appearance was a welcome moment for the Indians, for the small, oily fish were easy to catch and delicious. "On this page I have drawn the likeness of them as large as life," wrote Lewis, "it is as perfect as I can make it with my pen and will serve to give a general idea of the fish." The drawing did so, for it was one of the most meticulous and handsome of any entered in his journals. In this instance, Lewis also became an anatomist. He noted the "first bone of the gills next be hi[n]d the eye is of a bluis cast, and the second of a light goald colour nearly white." Little escaped his notice.

Water dripped from the roof slabs; smoke wafted from green logs burning on the hearth; men's voices echoed through the small fort. Occasionally arose the cry or voice of little Jean Baptiste Charbonneau. On February 11, 1806, he was a year old, a birthday not observed or noted, but a turning point in a young life when a child begins to walk and notice more of the world around him. The situation at the fort was one of weary, wet, and often sick men.

The lack of adequate, nutritious food was part of the problem, though exposure, chills, respiratory infections, and venereal diseases were more important causes. "Three Men were sent out hunting in order to try & kill some fowl or elk for the sick Men," wrote Joseph Whitehouse. Even though snow fell, the hunters had success and on February 17 reported that they had killed eight elk. That day the captains decided to close the salt operation, dispatching a patrol to the coast to retrieve the kettles and remaining supply of salt. Whitehouse reported that the going was tough for those headed to the saltworks. Sand, driven by wind, blasted their faces; rain fell, froze, and lashed at their exposed skin. The party had to wade creeks. Finally on February 21 the men closed the operation and turned around for the fort, returning after midnight in a tempest of rain.

The Corps of Discovery endured another month at Fort Clatsop, marking the days. On March 3, the growing impatience to get moving surfaced in Lewis's journal: "Every thing moves on in the old way and we are counting the days which separate us from the 1st of April and which bind us to Fort Clatsop." Lewis embarked on ornithological observations. He wrote about grouses, jays, magpies, mourning doves, herons, gulls, loons, fulmars, swans, ducks, and geese. This parade of feathered creatures kept him busy for nearly two weeks, though in off moments he continued treating the sick. McNeal and Goodrich he weaned from further doses of mercury for their venereal disease. To William Bratton, gripped with back pains, he "applied a bandage of flannel to the part and bathed and rubed it well with some vollatile linniment which I prepared with sperits of wine, camphor, castile soap, and a little laudinum."

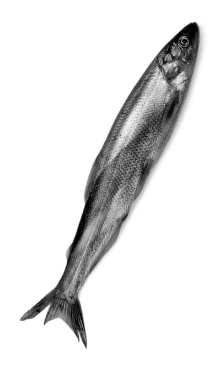

"We had a cloudy wet morning. I set out with 8 men and 4 hunters to bring the meat of the elk that had been killed, which was at a greater distance from the fort than any we had yet brought in. There is a large river that flows into the southeast part of Hayley's Bay, upon which, about 20 miles from its mouth, our hunters discovered falls, which had about 60 feet of perpendicular pitch."
Patrick Gass, March 1, 1806
Left: Youngs Falls on Youngs River near Fort Clatsop, Oregon

Above: Candlefish, or smelt (Thaleichthys pacificus)

91

The treatment worked and within twenty-four hours Bratton was better and able to move about.

On March 16 the Coho salmon arrived in the river. A Clatsop Indian gigged one and brought it to the fort. Lewis measured the fish and found it two feet eight inches long and weighing ten pounds. Calling it the White Salmon Trout, he dutifully drew a likeness in his journal with the same detail as that expended on the eulachon. His penchant for counting remained undiminished. Lewis identified the numbers of rays on various fins. The arrival of this fish was a signal of the coming of spring and a time of food abundance for the Indians.

With each day that passed, the possibility of sending home scientific specimens, journals, and even a man or two from the party waned. The hunger for connection with maritime fur traders surfaced in the journals of both Lewis and Clark. Jefferson had sparked this interest in his 1803 letter of instructions to Lewis: "On your arrival on that coast, endeavor to learn if there be any port within your reach frequented by sea-vessels of any nation, and to send two of your trusty people back by sea, in such way as shall appear practicable, with a copy of your notes."

Eagerly the captains interviewed the local Indians and, as best they could render phonetic spellings of the names, listed the known ship captains—Haley, Youens, Tallamon, Swipton, Moore, Mackey, Washington, Meship, Davidson, Jackson, Bolch, Skelley, and Callallamet—a trader with a wooden leg. None appeared, and though they speculated that the traders probably had a port of call where they may have wintered over, the captains could gain no definitive information about such a site.

Preparations for departure quickened. Two of the dugouts that had cracked were pegged and repaired. The captains sought diligently to acquire Chinook canoes to supplement their small flotilla. The bartering did not go well; the prices of canoes were high. "One handkerchief would contain all the Small articles of merchandize which we possess," wrote Clark. "The ballance of the Stock Consists of 6 Small blue robes or Blankets one of Scarlet. one uniform Artillerist's Coat and hat, 5 robes made of our larg flag, and a fiew our old Clothes trimed with ribon." This slim inventory the party had to hold in reserve, for its only hope of obtaining horses and crossing part of the Columbia Plateau by land hinged on the power of these items. The Clatsop canoe did not come into the possession of the party by trade, but Drouillard had success in bartering for one from the Cathlamet. He traded away Lewis's laced, uniform coat and a dried half carrot measure of tobacco. "It seems that nothing excep this coat would induce them to dispose of a canoe," wrote Lewis, "which in their mode of traffic is an article of the greatest val[u]e except a wife, with whom it is equal." He concluded: "I think the U' States are indebted to me another Uniform coat, for that of which I have disposed on this occasion was but little woarn."

When it was clear that the Clatsops would not sell a canoe, the captains agreed to stealing one. This moral lapse and violation of equitable dealing was excused on the grounds that the Indians had made off with at least six elk killed by the hunters during the winter. Ordway wrote that four men stole a canoe and hid it near the fort, "as we are in want of it." The theft was a discomforting closing note to a sojourn of more than four months among the Lower Chinookans.

The time to leave was at hand. The winter on the North Pacific Coast had produced momentous consequences. The expedition had established the first American military presence in the region; Fort Clatsop became a bargaining chip in the diplomatic contest for control of the vast Oregon Country. In a very real sense, the descent of the Columbia, the exploration of its estuary, the construction and occupancy of the fort, and the assessment of the Native peoples and the resources of the land fixed national interest on the distant shores of the North Pacific. From this point to the Oregon Treaty of 1846, there was no turning back. The United States had embarked on the path of building a transcontinental empire.

"I have a view of the Coast for an amence distance to the S.E. by S. the nitches and points of high land which forms this Corse for a long ways aded to the inoumerable rocks of emence Sise out at a great distance from the Shore and against which the Seas brak with great force gives this Coast a most romantic appearance."

William Clark, January 8, 1806

Left: Ecola with Haystack Rock rising through the mist, Cannon Beach, Oregon

The last evening Shabono and his Indian woman was very impatient to be permitted to go with me, and was therefore indulged; She observed that She had traveled a long way with us to See the great waters, and that now the monstrous fish was also to be Seen, She thought it verry hard that She could not be permitted to See either. William Clark, January 6, 1806

Above: Indian women and partially butchered whale, coast of Washington (Edward S. Curtis)

"I proceeded on about 2 miles to near the base of high Mountain where I found our Salt makers, and with them Sergt. Gass, Geo. Shannon was out in the woods assisting Jo Field and gibson to kill Some meat, the Salt makers had made a neet Close Camp, Convenient to wood Salt water and the fresh water of the Clât Sop river which at this place was within 100 paces of the Ocian"

William Clark, January 7, 1805

Above: Sea anemone, a colorful occupant of Pacific tidepools

Right: Salt marsh at Willapa Bay near Long Beach, Washington

Up the Great Columbia

"There is a beautiful prairie and a number of ponds below the mouth of Sandy river; and about two miles from the Columbia the soil is rich with white cedar timber, which is very much stripped of its bark, the natives making use of it both for food and clothing." Patrick Gass, April 5, 1806

Anticipation grew as signs of spring swept across the mouth of the Columbia River. In March 1806, the Corps of Discovery watched eagerly for a break in the weather and confirmation that it was time to start moving up the river. Expectations marked the days. Nearly five months had passed since the captains and their crew had arrived on the shore of the Pacific—no ship had entered the harbor, and no prospect arose for sending specimens, journals, or even a man or two from their ranks home by sea. To leave one or two men to wait for a vessel received consideration, but the captains dismissed the idea, for the strategy on the return was to break up the force into smaller units and achieve specific exploring objectives. The expedition could not afford a reduction in its ranks. The trick became finding harbingers of spring. To Patrick Gass it was the sighting of a new generation of mosquitoes on March 14. For Lewis and Clark the best sign was the arrival of coho salmon two days later, confirmation of the great fish runs and quickening of life in the empire of the Columbia.

Preparations for departure intensified. The weeks of hunting, tanning, and working with elk hides had paid off. The men had manufactured 358 pairs of moccasins and a personal cache of patch leather for every member of the expedition. Lewis had written copiously and productively in his journals; Clark copied most of the entries into his set of notebooks. Clark had completed the draft of his map of the American West and had worked on smaller maps illustrating details observed along the way. The captains had also prepared summary itineraries by date, mile, and feature, and assembled miscellaneous notes to buttress their primary journals.

Departing activities included issuing a "certificate of good deportment" to the Clatsop headman Delashewilt. The captains appended the names of the Corps of Discovery to this document, suspecting that when the chief showed it to a sea captain, it would confirm their success in crossing the continent. They also posted a copy of the document in the officers' quarters at Fort Clatsop. Lewis wrote:

> The object of this list is, that through the medium of some civilized person who may see the same, it may be made known to the informed world, that the party consisting of the persons whose names are hereunto annexed, and who were sent out by the government of the U'States in May 1804 to explore the interior of the Continent of North America, did penetrate the same by way of the Missouri and Columbia Rivers, to the discharge of the latter into the Pacific Ocean, where they arrived on the 14th November 1805, and from whence they departed the [blank] day of March 1806 on their return to the United States by the same rout they had come out.

On the back of the sheet they sketched a map showing the upper Missouri and Columbia Rivers and the "track we had Come and that we meant to pursue on our return," noted Lewis. And then as triple insurance of leaving a trace of their sojourn, the captains gave Chief Com-com-mo-ly of the Chinooks a like certificate and list of the expedition's personnel.

On March 19 Lewis entered a lengthy essay on the personal appearance, clothing, and adornment of the Natives in the vicinity. His notes were like a photomural of the dozens of individuals who had visited Fort Clatsop, each leaving a personal portrait that he now blended into a remarkable group picture. The "penetrating eye of the amorite," a strange phrase that Lewis here employed to describe his furtive glances at partially

Left: Harbinger of spring, western trillium or wake-robin (Trillium ovatum). Collected on April 10, 1806 in the Columbia Gorge.

clothed Native women, surfaced in his commentary. Awkwardly he described the women's robe and noted: "when this vest is woarn the breast of the woman is concealed, but without it which is almost always the case, they are exposed, and from the habit of remaining loose and unsuspended grow to great length particularly in aged women in many of whom I have seen the bubby reach as low as the waist." Clark included part of the discussion on female anatomy in his copy and skipped the remainder.

Thwarted several times by weather but unwilling to remain to the end of the month as planned, the Corps of Discovery on March 23 spent a hectic morning packing, dividing cargo, distributing canisters and weapons, loading jerked meat, smoked eulachon, and other meager foodstuffs, and preparing to depart. The moment differed dramatically from the tally of supplies that had gone into the keelboat and pirogues at Wood River in May 1804. Then the men had loaded one hundred gallons of whiskey and kegs of flour, corn, pork, sugar, biscuits, beans, "portable soup," lard, a bag of coffee beans, beads, twists of tobacco, and candlewicks. In special packages the captains had carried gifts of trade beads, handkerchiefs, mirrors, peace medals, and American flags to cement diplomatic ties between the leaders of numerous tribes and the United States. At Fort Clatsop the primary provisions were jerked elk meat and salt. The diminishing supply of trade goods had cut off the flow of wapato, salal berries, and other local commodities offered by the Clatsops and Chinooks. Their remaining trade goods, as Clark ruefully admitted, were little more than a miscellany of red and white beads and fishhooks. Their treasury was bankrupt, but the herbarium sheets of botanical specimens, examples of Indian basketry and weaponry, pelts of mammals, and skins of birds were a treasure of a greater sort. Most precious of all were their journals and maps, sealed in lead canisters to protect them from moisture. Hundreds of thousands of words documented their daily life and, more importantly, the land, peoples, and resources of the American West.

As on their departures from Camp Dubois and Fort Mandan, the Corps carried its weapons, scientific instruments, axes, files, chisels, and the books they used in the field. The library—the first in the watersheds of the Missouri and Columbia—was critical to the scientific objectives of the expedition. The titles included Patrick Kelly's *A Practical Introduction to Sperhics and Nautical Astronomy* (London, 1796); Antoine Simon Le Page du Pratz's *History of Louisiana* (London, 1774); Richard Kirwan's *Elements of Mineralogy* (London, 1784); John Miller's *An Illustration of the Sexual System of Linnaeus* (1779 and 1789); and Benjamin Smith Barton's *Elements of Botany* (Philadelphia, 1803). From these volumes the captains drew instruction in navigation, natural history, and general knowledge. There were neither Bibles nor novels in the baggage; what the party carried was what was essential for daily existence and for the missions laid out by President Jefferson. Religious, philosophical, and fictional essays were the fare of civilized society but not of the camps of the Corps of Discovery.

The expedition departed on March 23. "At 1 P.M.," wrote Lewis, "we bid a final adieu to Fort Clatsop." The men and the Charbonneau family were squeezed into three large and two small canoes. The large canoes, the patched and leaking dugouts, were the product of labors at Canoe Camp on the Clearwater. The two small ones were of local manufacture: one purchased from the Cathlamets, the other "appropriated" from the Clatsops. At the eleventh hour Delashewilt and some twenty other Indians showed up to sell a canoe. "We did not purchase it," wrote Lewis tersely, though the party managed to barter for one more sea otter pelt. The men paddled nineteen miles and camped at the mouth of a tidal slough entering the Columbia upstream from Tongue Point, where some of the hunters killed two elk.

Tides and currents beset the travelers, often compelling them to wait several hours. In March the Columbia was high. Its waters, fed by the constant rains of winter in the Coast Range, Cascades, and distant Rockies, surged in muddy flood over the lowlands

"The Deer of this Coast differ materially from our Common deer in a much as they are much darker deeper bodied Shorter ledged horns equally branched from the beem the top of the tail black from the rute to the end Eyes larger and do not lope but jump." William Clark, November 19, 1805
Above: Jumping deer

"The interior part of the island is praries and ponds, with a heavy growth of Cottonwood ash and willow near the river. we have seen more waterfowl on this island than we have previously seen since we left Fort Clatsop, consisting of geese, ducks, large swan, and Sandhill crains." Meriwether Lewis, March 28, 1806
Right: Wetland in the spring rain, Puget Island, Washington

and inundated much of the land. The high water was but a portent, however, of the spring freshets that, with melting snows, would surge down its course in June toward the sea.

When the expedition approached Puget and Tenas Illahe Islands, the Native sturgeon fishery was in full operation. The Wahkiakum and Cathlamet bands took advantage of the deep channels on the margins of the islands to fish by trolling from their canoes. "They had ten or a douzen very fine sturgeon," wrote Lewis. "We offered to purchase some of their fish but they asked us such an extravagent price that we declined purchase." The expedition paddled on, wending its way shore to shore, following the main channel of the Columbia. On March 27 it reached the mouth of the Cowlitz. The Skil-loots who lived in the vicinity were particularly friendly. They gave the travelers dried smelt, sturgeon, wapato, camas, and other roots. "Most of the party were served by the natives with as much as they could eat," wrote Lewis. "They insisted on our remaining all day with them and hunting the Elk which they informed us were very abundant in their neighbouhood," but the Corps did not tarry. Conditions were unfavorable for drying and repairing their canoes and they sought a better location.

The islands of the Columbia estuary abounded in wildlife. Both Columbian black-tailed and white-tailed deer shared this habitat, as did a variety of birds, reptiles, and amphibians. Lewis and Clark sent hunters ashore at Deer Island. The men sighted more than a hundred deer and killed seven. "We have seen more waterfowl on this island than we have previously seen since we left Fort Clatsop," noted Lewis. "Joseph Fields informed me that Vultures had draged a large buck which he had killed about 30 yards, had skined it and broken the back bone." The birds, possibly condors, ate four of the deer before the hunters could retrieve the kills and carry them to camp. Deer Island was also the habitat of garter snakes—bundles of them writhing in clutches of forty or fifty. Patrick Gass, a bit unnerved, confessed that he had never seen so many snakes in one place in his life. Lewis secured a specimen and began counting. He found "160 scuta on the abdomen and 71 on the tail." As ever, little escaped his scrutiny.

Signs of spring appeared daily. The elk began shedding their horns. Birds sang at daybreak in the thickets along the river. Tender, green leaves started to unfold on the thimbleberry, and the salmonberry thrust dark, red-colored shoots out of the ground (edible much like asparagus if steamed in a rock-lined oven). In swampy ground the brilliant yellow flowers of skunk cabbage, each the size of a flour scoop, rose above a cluster of dark green, stinking leaves. Frogs croaked at dusk in the wetlands along the river. The pink-flowering currant broke into bloom and, like a magnet, drew visiting hummingbirds. Spring was the quickening of new life and hinted at the promise of the land. The weather reflected the pulsing changes with blasts of wind and rain, moments of intense sunlight, and gatherings of dark clouds.

At Cathlapootle, the village of fourteen lodges at the mouth of the Lewis River, the explorers found the Indians replenishing food supplies. They had already exploited the eulachon runs. The rafters of their houses were filled with strings of dried, smoked smelt, while the most recent catch hung from small sticks lined through their gills in the early process of curing. These people had both fresh sturgeon and wapato, an opportunity for bartering. Lewis offered fresh deer hides from the previous day's hunt. He purchased a dozen dogs and supplies of roots.

Continuing east, the expedition passed Wappato Island, Image Canoe Island, and Diamond Island and, on the last day of March, put ashore at a large prairie upstream from the mouth of Seal River (Washougal), at the mouth of which large numbers of harbor seals congregated. The setting was stunning: a great bottomland of hundreds of acres of meadows and cottonwoods with swampy lakes, along the north bank of the Columbia. Subsequent parties of fur trappers sojourned there and called it Prairie du The. On the south shore lay the delta of the Sandy River.

"The Sturgeon and a small fish like the Anchovy begin to run. they are taken in the Columbia about 50 mils. above us." Meriwether Lewis and William Clark, February, 1806

Left: Sturgeon (Acipenser medirostris)

Above: Arrowhead-shaped leaf of wapato (Sagittaria latifolia)

Awareness of probable food scarcity east of the Gorge drove the decision to camp at this site. The spring salmon runs had not yet reached this part of the river. The vast Columbia Plateau offered little prospect of game. "Under these circumstances," wrote Lewis, "there seems to be but a gloomy prospect for subsistence on any terms; we therefore took it into serious consideration what measures we were to pursue on this occasion." Timing was critical. The Corps of Discovery could not wait for the salmon runs, for the delay might mean a failure to connect with the Nez Perce, who would set out over the Lolo Trail as soon as the winter snows melted. Connection with the Nez Perce loomed critically, for they held the branded horses the expedition required to cross the Bitterroots. Camping at the entry to the Columbia Gorge was calculated to secure food supplies yet depart in time to reach the Nez Perce villages before they dispersed on their seasonal round.

In early April the captains agreed to camp for a week and scour the countryside. Some hunters were to seek game north of the Columbia, while others were dispatched to explore the south side of the Columbia and the Sandy River. Lewis and Clark had concluded in 1805 that the Sandy was the primary drainage of the open country that lay to the south. In 1806 they began to revise their perception. To test the hypothesis they dispatched Sergeant Nathaniel Pryor and two men in a small canoe on April 1, to explore the "Quicksand River" as far as they could ascend. Pryor reported that the Sandy was a small stream. He and his party ascended it approximately six miles to a point where it divided and was less than six feet deep.

While Pryor and his patrol were out, several canoes filled with hungry Indian families passed the base camp. "They inform us," wrote Clark, "that they reside at the great rapids and that their relations at that place were much Streightened for the want of food; that they had consumed their winter Store of dryed fish and those of the present Season had not yet arived." Further confirmation that times were tough was the comment: "They informed us that the nativs above them were in the Same Situation, and that they did not expect the Salmon to arrive untill the full of the next moon which happens on the 2nd of May." This intelligence only deepened the concern of the captains about what lay ahead and redoubled their commitment to try to stock up on foodstuffs before passing through the Gorge and facing new challenges. In the evening the hunters who had worked along the south shore returned. They had killed four elk and two deer; those on the north side, however, while sighting both elk and deer, had not had any luck. The captains wrote in their journals about their hopes to purchase horses by trading away their canoes and, as soon as they could, set out by land. They speculated that when they reached the Snake, "we propose sending a party of four or five men a head to collect our horses that they may be in readiness for us by our arrival at the Choppunish." A double supply of horses—those used for crossing the Plateau and those at the Nez Perce villages for crossing the Bitterroots—would insure both a means of travel and a food supply. "We now view the horses," wrote Lewis, "as our only certain resource for food, nor do we look forward to it with any destestation or horrow, so soon is the mind occupied with any interesting object reconciled to it's situation."

Indians of the Shah-ha-lah village, including two identified as Cash-hooks, visited the camp and apprised the explorers of the presence of a large river whose entrance lay among islands along the south shore. When they sketched it with charcoal on a mat, Clark decided to hire a Cash-hook guide and explore its lower reaches. He set out with six men in a dugout to retrace the route downstream. They stopped at the Shah-ha-lah village; the inhabitants were shy, if not sulky, and refused to sell any wapato. Clark then performed some of his tricks—moving the needle of the compass with a magnet and setting a fire with a match that caught ablaze and burned brightly, changing its color. This "astonished and alarmed these natives and they laid Several parsles of Wappato at my feet," he wrote, and begged him to put out the bad fire, which soon extinguished itself. Clark then lit his pipe and shared it with those who

had provided wapato. "They appeared Somewhat passified," he wrote, and he paddled on in search of the elusive river.

The great Willamette, the largest tributary of the lower Columbia, was precisely where the Cash-hooks had sketched. It flowed quietly into the Columbia at the upper end of Wappato (Sauvie) Island and was approximately one-third the size of the great river of the West. Its entrance had eluded the explorers. This time, however, Clark turned into its main channel at a point where he could see Mounts Jefferson, Hood, St. Helens, and Rainier on the horizon. Clark identified the stream as the Multnomah, a name identical to a village on the north side of Wappato Island. "The Current of the Multnomar is as jentle as that of the Columbia," he wrote. The river was promising, for by Clark's assessment it was "Sufficiently deep for the largest Ship." With a five-fathom cord he found that for nearly a third of its width he was unable to hit bottom.

Clark and his party paddled upstream approximately eight miles to a spot where they found an unoccupied lodge so filled with fleas that they dared not sleep in it. The occupants had but recently left, he presumed, for the fishery at Willamette Falls; the house contained mats, bladders filled with oil, baskets, bowls, wood trenchers, and other possessions. The structure, located on the northeast bank of the Willamette, measured thirty by forty feet. Clark remained impressed and wrote: "I think the wedth of the river may be Stated at 500 yards and Sufficenttly deep for a Man of War of any burthen." Clark and his detachment rejoined Lewis near the mouth of the Washougal on April 3 to discover that efforts to build up food supplies had not fared well.

The following day Sergeant Gass and his party brought in bear meat and venison. They reported having killed six deer and an elk but had found the flesh so meager on the poor animals that they had not deemed it worthwhile to try to carry their kills back to camp. When Fields and Drouillard returned with two deer, the captains dispatched them up the Columbia to join other hunters in the bottomlands along the south shore. Prospects improved a bit on April 5 when some of the hunters carried in four elk killed by Sergeant Ordway. "It had been so illy dryed that we feared it would not keep," wrote Lewis. "We therefore directed it to be cut thinner and redryed over a fire this evening." The men also brought in three bear cubs, having failed to find their mother. The Indians fancied the cubs as pets and traded wapato for them.

The expedition resumed its eastward course on April 6. Hunters had killed three elk and wounded two others, so the captains headed to shore and ordered the men to build pole frames and fires, cut the meat into strips, and spend the night preserving the meat. "This Supply of Elk," wrote Clark, "I think by useing economey and in addition of roots and dogs which we may probably precure from [t]he Nativs on Lewis's river will be Sufficient to last us to the Chopunnish where we Shall Meet with our horses." While the elk meat steamed over the fires, the men refurbished their guns, calibrated the gun sights, and prepared for the challenges of the portages ahead.

The Columbia is a river of moods. It can flow swiftly and quietly, or turn into a wave-chopped sea when whipped by winds sweeping east or west through its great gorge. Just as the Corps was ready to press on, the winds came up and "blew So hard and raised the Waves So emensely high from the N.E.," wrote Clark, "and tossed our Canoes against the Shore in such a manner as to render it necessary to haul them up on the bank." Again the party played the waiting game. John Shields, the skilled gunsmith, worked on Clark's small rifle. Clark passed the hours writing in his journal about the numerous aged Indians in the villages he had visited who were blind, perhaps, he thought, because of their constant exposure to the sun and water. Lewis walked three miles down the riverbank and, when he found a blooming salmonberry bush, revised his discussion of the plant. His entry was interesting, for he invoked the classification system of Linnaeus, the Swedish botanist. "This bryer," wrote Lewis, "is of the class Polyandria and order Polygynia." Neither the captains nor the men experienced idle hours.

"Some of the cliffs is 200 feet high. on the tops of those hills the land is excessively rich and thickly timbered with different Species of Fir intermixed with white cedder. I Saw one of the Fir trees which is 100 and 4 feet in length." John Ordway, April 5, 1806
Left: Ancient basalt flows sculpted by the Columbia River at Cape Horn, Washington

Above: Cape Horn from the bank of the Columbia about 1910 (Albert Barnes) (Maryhill Museum, Maryhill, Washington)

Once the winds subsided, the Corps renewed its journey. The men paddled against the current and stopped at the Wah-cle-lah village, west of Beacon Rock. The Upper Chinookans were "very unfriendly" and "illy disposed," though they sold wapato and five dogs to the travelers. Late in the day the expedition reached the Clah-cle-lah village near the Lower Cascades and, again, the diarists wrote about the "sulky and illdisposed" nature of the people. The village was large and gave evidence of an even greater population in previous years. Lewis counted fourteen plank and bark-covered lodges, the locations of nine structures that had been removed, and traces of ten to a dozen more. What the captains did not appear to grasp was that the residents of Wah-cle-lah and Clah-cle-lah were arbiters of the portage. In subsequent years they demanded tribute from fur trappers crossing their trails around the rapids. Neither Lewis nor Clark understood that they had trespassed in crossing the portage the previous October, nor that they might be expected to pay for the passage when they used it a second time.

Nevertheless, Lewis was delighted with the results of a visit to the Clah-cle-lah village. A man offered to sell the pelt of a mountain goat. "Nothing could have been more acceptable than the animal itself," wrote Lewis. "The skin of the head of the sheep [goat] with the horns remaining was cased in such a manner as to fit the head of a man by whom it was woarn and highly prized as an ornament." Lewis paid two elk-skins and a knife to obtain this specimen. The Natives explained that the goats lived on the cliffs towering above the rapids, and that the pelts in the village were the result of a recent hunting expedition. The next three days were consumed with arduous labor and danger, for the Columbia ran nearly twenty feet higher than the previous fall. The Cascades—a series of three major rapids in less than six miles—surged over boulders that made the upriver transit almost impossible. The Corps first tried to hug the south shore and pass via a small channel between Bradford Island and the south bank. This route proved impossible. On April 10, on the north bank, the men began the arduous task of cordelling the canoes up through the rapids.

For hours the men dragged the vessels upstream. Spring rains only added to their misery. They used elk-hide ropes and fought the dugouts through the currents, scrambling over the slippery boulders along the shore, tugging and hefting, passing the line from man to man and cursing the force of the current tearing against their efforts. "One of the men lamed one of his feet towing over the Stons," noted John Ordway. Drouillard and the Fields brothers, who had gone ahead with a small canoe, got it through the Middle Cascades, then lost it when their towing rope broke. The vessel swept downstream but was rescued by the Indians below, who returned it and received payment of two knives. The intent of other Natives was far more combative. One threw stones down the bank where the men struggled with the canoes. Another tried to kidnap Lewis's Newfoundland dog and had led it off nearly half a mile when he was detected, pursued, and compelled to abandon his mission.

At this point, midway up the rapids but facing the worst and largest set, the captains ordered the men to unload the baggage and carry all up to the trail where they established a guarded portage camp. The rains continued. "All of the party except a fiew to guard the baggage turned out with Capt. Clark," wrote Ordway, "to takeing up our canoes with the tow Rope up the big Shoote." It took all morning to get two vessels through the Upper Cascades. The men then went back to the baggage cache, ate lunch, and renewed the task, again bringing up two canoes, one by water and the smallest overland. "The most of the mens feet sore towing over the Sharp rocks," noted Ordway.

As soon as the party passed into the great backwater above the Cascades landslide, Lewis went to the Y-eh-huh village, friendly people living in eleven lodges, where he bartered with the hides of elk and deer for two small canoes and four paddles. The expedition then set out, mostly hugging the north shore and passing

"On our way to this village we passed several beautifull cascades which fell from a great hight over the stupendious rocks which cloles the river on both sides nearly . . . the most remarkable of these casscades falls about 300 feet perpendicularly over a solid rock into a narrow bottom of the river on the south side."

Meriwether Lewis,
April 9, 1806

Right: Multnomah Falls, Oregon

through "very romantic scenes" where, as Lewis noted, "some handsome cascades are seen on either hand tumbling from the stupendious rocks of the mountains into the river." The Corps passed through the transition from coast to plateau, marked by the appearance of pines and the advent of circular, subterranean lodges, and mat shelters.

At each village where they saw horses, the captains' eagerness for trade mounted. Paddling against the current seemed poor gain when, instead, they might barter for horses, abandon their canoes, and set out across the plateau. Each effort to exchange their meager trade goods failed to secure mounts. They made three vain attempts on April 15, before settling in at Rock Fort Camp at the mouth of Mill Creek, at the eastern entrance to the Gorge. Clark took off the next morning with nine men and Sacagawea, to visit the villages along the north shore between there and the Long Narrows to try to trade for horses. Lewis sent out hunters, collected a variety of plants, and set other men to work making packsaddles and horse harnesses from elk hide.

Clark did his best at the Skil-loot village, where he had promises of trade. Cruzatte played his fiddle; the men danced. "I rose early after a bad nights rest," wrote Clark, "and took my merchindize to a rock which afforded an elegable Situation for my purpose, and at a Short distance from the houses, and divided the articles of merchindize into parsels of Such articles as I thought best Calculated to pleas the Indians." The prospects faded after hours of looking and near deals. Clark smarted from the frustrations. Twice he invoked the word "tanterlised" when describing how he felt about the unwillingness of the Indians to part with their horses. Then, trying to win a bit of favor, he played the role of doctor and treated the chief's sores. Clark's frame of mind, however, surfaced in his journal when he wrote about treating the chief's wife, "a Sulky Bitch," who complained of back pains. "This I thought a good oppertunity to get her on my Side," he wrote, "giveing here Something for her back." He rubbed camphor on her temples and back and applied a layer of warm flannel. This convinced the woman that she was nearly restored. Clark finally sent word back to Lewis that all was for naught.

Simple logic dictated the need for horses. If the captains could put some of the men on shore, they could abandon the larger, heavier dugouts and move more quickly. The slower the expedition moved, the more it would have to spend its meager goods for food and firewood. Survival, it seemed, hinged on escaping from the river and speeding up the journey to the Bitterroots. Lewis impatiently sent word to Clark to double the price offered. At last, on April 17, Clark purchased three horses, and Charbonneau obtained another.

Lewis caught up with Clark at the Skil-loot village near the foot of the Long Narrows. Here the party had to portage, but because of the tremendous rise in the river, the enterprise was far longer than when descending the Columbia. The four horses enabled the men to abandon the two remaining dugouts. One of these faithful craft—battered, patched, and pitched—fell beneath the axe to become firewood. The expedition now proceeded to pull the five small canoes up the rapids, while some of the men and the horses carried the baggage along the north shore.

The expedition at this point passed through the greatest concentration of Native peoples living along the Columbia River. As the portage proceeded, Lewis wrote on April 19: "There was great joy with the natives last night in consequence of the arrival of the salmon; one of those fish was caught; this was the harbinger of good news to them." The lean weeks of winter were almost at an end. Life now quickened, for the fishery would bring hard labor and trade. Lewis, without realizing it, also obliquely described the critical "first salmon" rites, noting: "This fish was dressed and being divided into small peices was given to each child in the village. this custom is founded in a supersticiouis opinon that it will hasten the arrival of the salmon."

"Their women as well as those of the 3 villages next below us pierce the cartelage of the nose and insert various ornaments. they very seldom imprint any figures on their skins; a few I observed had one or two longitudinal lines of dots on the front of the leg, reaching from the ankle upwards about midleg." Meriwether Lewis, April 11, 1806

Left: Pictographs and petroglyphs near Wishram, Washington

The good news of the salmon was joined by the success of more hard trading. Lewis and Clark bartered two of their brass kettles, along with other goods, and closed a deal for four more horses. "We have now only one small kettle to a mess of 8 men," wrote Lewis. The horses were restless. Alexander Willard allowed one to walk away and it was lost. Lewis was furious: "I repremanded him more severely for this peice of negligence than had been usual with me," he wrote. He ordered the remaining horses hobbled and guarded throughout the night. All except one were uncastrated stallions and, as Lewis remarked, "this is a season at which they are most vicious."

The portage at The Dalles and Celilo Falls required patience, hard work, sharp trading, and vigilance. The residents of this region were accustomed to visitors and knew how to profit by their innocence and negligence. Petty thefts bedeviled the party at a time when it could ill afford to lose any possessions. The Indians made off with five or six tomahawks and some utensils. When Lewis caught a man trying to steal an iron socket for a canoe pole, he struck him and ordered him out of the camp, threatening with oaths that he would kill them all and set fire to their houses. Fortunately Lewis's tirade was beyond translation, though its intent must surely have been clear.

Near the mouth of the Deschutes River, the captains divided the party. One group would proceed ahead with horses and baggage by land; another would follow later in the day; the men in the remaining canoes would proceed via the river. Now the challenges would be lack of firewood, bitterly cold camps with a single cooking fire, hard walking through sand and rocks, straying horses, and a diet largely restricted to roots and dog meat. Fate played into the party's hands when a Nez Perce man and his family and thirteen head of horses caught up with them on their journey home. Although the captains hesitated, they eventually leased three of his herd and purchased a few more along the way. Thus, a short distance above the John Day River, the party was ready to travel entirely by land. When the efforts to barter away the last canoes failed, Lewis ordered Drouillard to start chopping up the craft. He struck one and cut off a piece sufficient to persuade the Indians to trade. The captains thus sold the last two canoes for a few strands of beads and set out along the north bank.

On April 27, warmly received by Chief Yel-lept, the captains learned of a good overland route that cut from the mouth of the Walla Walla to the confluence of the Clearwater and Snake Rivers. The Indians advised that the trail provided wood, deer and antelope, and a shortcut that saved more than eighty miles compared to following the banks of the lower Snake. Yel-lept presented Clark with a handsome white horse, hoping to receive a kettle. None could be spared. Clark, however, gave the chief his officer's sword, one hundred lead balls, and some powder. Clearly the expedition had established a firm relationship with the Native peoples in that vicinity. Also helpful was the discovery of a Shoshone woman, a prisoner, with whom it was possible to open a circuitous translation via Sacagawea and Charbonneau. Lewis wrote: "we Conversed with them for Several hours and fully Satisfy all their enquiries with respect to our Selves and the Object of our pursute. they were much pleased."

As had been the occasion on previous days crossing the Plateau, the captains were called upon to act as doctors. As would-be doctors, they carried much magic; in some instances their medical practices would serve to obtain food, firewood, or horses. Yel-lept's band brought in several who needed medical help. The cases varied from rheumatism to a broken arm. Lewis and Clark gave eyewash to those with sore eyes; they splinted and trussed the broken arm and put it in a sling. In the evening, the large throng of Indians gathered to hear the fiddle and watch the men of the Corps of Discovery dance. Then the Indians—some 350 of them—sang and danced. "At 10 P.M. the dance ended," wrote Lewis, "and the nativs retired; they were much gratified in Seeing Some of our Party join them in their dance."

"They also purchase Silk grass, of which they make their nets & Sales for takeing fish   they also purchase Bear grass and maney other things for their fish." Meriwether Lewis, April 20, 1806

Right: The fisherman Wishham, 1909 (Edward S. Curtis)

112

"I walked on Shore with Shabono on the N. Side through a handsom bottom. met Several parties of women and boys in Serch of herbs & roots to Subsist on maney of them had parcels of the Stems of the Sun flower."

William Clark, April 14, 1806

The next morning the Indians loaned the explorers canoes to cross to the south bank of the Columbia. They swam their horses over, loaded their slender store of supplies, weapons, and baggage onto the pack saddles, and set out for Nez Perce country. The journey home by land had begun. Just a little over a month had elapsed since saying their farewells to the Clatsops and Chinooks at Fort Clatsop. Ahead lay the difficult Bitterroots. No doubt questions passed through the minds of the men as they stood on the shore of the Columbia, about to leave its familiar waters. Had the Nez Perce maintained their horses during the winter? How deep were the snows on the mountains? Could they possibly get to St. Louis before the onset of winter would hold them captive on the frozen plains? Everything depended on the answers to these troubling questions.

Left: Balsamroots (Balsamorhiza) collected April 14, 1806, along the Columbia River below The Dalles, Oregon

"The fir has been lately injured by a fire near this place and many of them have discharged considerable quantities of rozin." Meriwether Lewis, April 9, 1806

Above: Fire-damaged tree

"Labiech killed 14 Goose & a Brant, Collins one
Jos. Fields & R 3   those gees are much Smaller than
Common, and have white under their rumps
& around the tale"

William Clark, November 2, 1805

Above: Canadian geese (Branta canadensis)

"Weather warm; the sweet willow & white oak begin to put forth their leaves."
Meriwether Lewis and William Clark, April 17, 1806
Right: Sunset on the Columbia

The Formidable Bitterroots

"Having exhausted all our merchandize we are obliged to have recourse to every subterfuge in order to prepare in the most ample manner in our power to meet that wretched portion of our journy, the Rocky Mountain, where hungar and cold in their most rigorous forms assail the waried traveller."

Meriwether Lewis, June 2, 1806

The Corps of Discovery encountered the promise of the eastern Columbia Plateau in the watersheds of the Walla Walla, Touchet, and Tucannon Rivers. South of the confluence of the Snake and Columbia, the countryside lay like great sea billows. Rolling hills stretched to the southern horizon and the snow-covered Blue Mountains. Sagebrush and bunch grasses clothed the land. Horse-high rye grass—*Waiilatpu* in the Cayuse language—grew rank in the bottoms along the rivers. Towering cottonwoods scented the air with sweetness, inspiring later generations to refer to them as Balm of Gilead trees. Swampy meadows lay like ponds painted by blue camas flowers. Patches of cow parsnip thrived in the wetlands and provided nourishment to hungry Native peoples—and even to visitors. Lewis noted: "I tasted of this plant and found it agreeable and eat heartily of it without feeling any inconvenience."

Freedom from the constraints of the dugouts empowered the men. Now they could surmount the ridges, examine the country, and drive their eastward agenda with force. "The land of the plains," observed Lewis, "is much more fertile than below, less sand and covered with taller grass." Clark, too, admired the prospects. On the Tucannon, he wrote: "the land of good quality dark rich loam." Although the country was burned over, a legacy of Native fire ecology or the previous year's lightning storms, its prospect was inviting.

The journey was marked by rapid advances: twenty-six miles on May 1; twenty-eight miles on May 3. The party encountered scattered families of Natives. The first day out a contingent of Walla Wallas overtook the expedition to return a steel trap accidentally left with them. "I think we can justly affirm to the honor of these people," wrote Lewis, "that they are the most hospitable, honest and sincere that we have met with in our voyage." On May 3 the party encountered Nez Perce chief We-ark-koomt with ten young men. Identified by the explorers as "Chief Bighorn" because of the horn he wore strapped to his left arm, he had descended the Snake in advance of the expedition the previous fall to prepare the villages ahead for the visitors. The Nez Perce were now to accompany the Corps of Discovery to the Bitterroot Mountains. On May 4 the men met Te-toh-ar-sky, the younger of the Nez Perce chiefs who had traveled with them to the great falls of the Columbia. The Nez Perce encouraged the exploring party to cross the Snake, ascend its north bank, and follow the north bank of the Clearwater above its confluence. "We determined to take the advice of the Indians," noted Lewis.

On May 5 the expedition reached the mouth of the Koos-koos-kee (Clearwater). Although several villages of Indians resided in the vicinity, there was little food available for purchase. Most of the people had dispersed to harvest camas and escape the lean times of early spring. The exigencies of survival preyed on all. Lewis and Clark, desperate to barter, reverted to cheap tricks as medical charlatans. Clark bartered a "phial of eye-water" for a gray mare. His success in exchanging "medical services" for food stemmed from the fortuitous application of liniment on the lame leg of a man in the same vicinity the previous year. "My friend Capt. C. is their favorite phisician," wrote Lewis, "and has already received many applications." While the matter of deception bulked large, Lewis excused it by claiming that circumstances made the ruse pardonable since "our stock is now reduced to a mere handfull."

"We again proceeded N. 45 E. 3 M. through the high plain to a small creek 5 yds wide branch of the Kimooenem C. this stream falls into the creek some miles below. the hills of this creek like those of the Kimooenem are high it's bottoms narrow and possess but little timber, lands of a good quality, a dark rich loam. we continued our rout up this creek, on it's N. side N. 75 E. 7 Ms." Meriwether Lewis, May 3, 1806

Left: Pataha Creek near Pomeroy, Washington, on the overland shortcut from Wallula Gap on the Columbia to the Clearwater River

Clark was troubled by the trickery but provided a slippery excuse: "We take Care to give them no article which Can possibly injure them."

At this Nez Perce village, Lewis displayed his prickly personality. Easily provoked, he was consuming a supper of dog meat when a tense moment erupted at the campfire:

> while at dinner an indian fellow verry impertinently threw a poor half starved puppy nearly into my plait by way of derision for our eating dogs and laughed very heartily at his own impertinence; I was so provoked at this insolence that I caught the puppy and th[r]ew it with great violence at him and struk him in the breast and face, siezed my tomahawk and shewed him by signs if he repeated his insolence I would tommahawk him, the fellow withdrew apparently much mortifyed and I continued my repast on dog without further molestation.

Lewis's public display of anger boiled over again when he discovered that some of the hunters had malingered in camp. Lewis chided them "for their indolence and inattention to the order of last evening." Hunger was probably a factor in the short tempers. It stalked the Corps of Discovery and the local Indians. Lewis observed that the Nez Perce had survived by consuming lichen, pine seeds, and the barely palatable inner bark of the trees. The men helped themselves to trout snared in an Indian trap, adding them to a solitary duck, horse meat, and four deer—the entire food supply for the party.

When the expedition arrived at the camp of Twisted Hair on May 8, the chief was sullen. A quarrel had simmered for weeks, if not months, over the management of the expedition's horses. Cutnose and other chiefs alleged that Twisted Hair was a two-faced old man, pretending to care for the captains' livestock but permitting their dispersal and hard use. Their criticisms had fired the man's intransigence. Equally disquieting was the report that spring runoff had caused the cave-in of the party's primary cache near Canoe Camp. The only solace was that the Indians had salvaged some of the saddles and canisters, but other valued possessions were lost. The captains faced days of recovering horses and supplies, sorting out rewards for services rendered, and sizing up whether or not to trust Twisted Hair as a friend.

The Nez Perce's homeland captivated Lewis:

> This country would form an extensive settlement; the climate appears quite as mild as that of similar latitude on the Atlantic coast if not more so and it cannot be otherwise than healthy; it possesses a fine dry pure air. the grass and many plants are now upwards of knee high. I have no doubt but this tract of country if cultivated would produce in great abundance every article essentially necessary to the comfort and subsistence of civilized man.

Patience paid off. Twisted Hair produced about half of the cached saddles. Other Nez Perce brought in twenty-one horses, most in good condition but five injured by too much riding. Three others suffered from sore backs, but, on the whole, the recovery of the livestock was a great boon to the expedition, for the horses helped insure the crossing of the Bitterroots—by carrying the party, or serving as food if other sources were not available. Within days the expedition secured the return of other mounts, until all but six were recovered (and two of those had gone with the Shoshone guide Toby and his son). Before the month passed, the captains would count all but two horses in their possession, a remarkable recovery of property and validation of trust extended by the Nez Perce.

On May 10 the expedition moved on sixteen miles through slippery snow to the vicinity of Kamiah—to the village of Tunnachemootoolt, a chief they had met the previous fall. He had an American flag flying on a staff near his principal lodge. The Nez Perce produced two bushels of camas, four cakes of cous roots, and a dried steelhead to feed the visitors. When the captains explained that they feared the consequences

"These indians are cruell horse-masters; they ride hard, and their saddles are so illy constructed that they cannot avoid wounding the backs of their horses . . . ."
Meriwether Lewis,
April 30, 1806

Right: Nez Perce saddle painted hide over frame (Nez Perce National Monument, Lapwai, Idaho)

of such a diet on the health of the party and wished to trade for horses to eat, the Indians would not barter. Instead, they insisted on giving two fat young horses to the captains as food. "This is a much greater act of hospitality than we have witnessed from any nation or tribe since we have passed the Rocky Mountains," wrote Lewis. He considered their generosity a hallmark of their "immortal honor."

Lewis and Clark distributed two more medals and, realizing that they had found the most important chiefs of the Nez Perce, concluded to hold a general council. Tunnachemootoolt (Broken Arm), Neehneparkheeook (Cutnose), Yoomparkkartim, and Hohats Illpilp, with many of their bands, assembled for the session. Lewis and Clark delivered the much-practiced speech that the United States was a powerful nation that sought to open trade with the tribes and restore peace and harmony among them. The message passed from English to French, then to Minataree and into Shoshone, and finally to Nez Perce. The protracted path of communication consumed half the day and then was sealed with the captains' special demonstrations of the power of magnetism, wonder of the telescope, awesome firing of the airgun, and a session of playing doctor.

The Nez Perce weighed the speech the following day in several hours of discussion. They then told the captains that by nature they were peaceful and had been driven to war only by the aggression of enemies. They explained that they had sent three men to smoke the peace pipe with the Shoshones of the Snake River, but all were murdered. Only then did they mount an expedition of retribution, killing forty-two Shoshones and losing but three of their party. They expressed willingness to cease such warfare.

The evening concluded with more gifts, including powder and balls, a small flag, and other articles, to the chiefs while Cutnose gave a horse to Drouillard. Lewis and Clark turned over the first of the promised guns with ammunition to Twisted Hair in payment for tending their horses over the winter. The captains then began soliciting the old man for the assistance of some of his grown sons as guides in crossing the mountains. To firm up the possibility, they invited Twisted Hair to move his family with them to the other side of the river where, for several weeks, the expedition would await the melting of the snow in the mountains.

Camp Choppunish, a site on the Clearwater River near present-day Kamiah, Idaho, became the third-longest point of residency for the expedition, exceeded only by the winters spent at Fort Mandan (North Dakota) and Fort Clatsop (Oregon). The location, an abandoned village in a meadow near the river, offered many attractions. It was secure and defensible, demarcated by an earthwork nearly thirty feet in diameter and rising three or four feet from the ground. Inside this the captains placed their baggage. Outside the ring the men constructed shelters of sticks and grass, resembling canvas wagon covers. The site lay adjacent to hunting grounds, including the high plains at the foot of the Bitterroots to the east. The camp lay on the banks of the river, where any day the salmon might appear, and from which the captains could gauge the melting of snow in the mountains. The bottom contained fine pasture for the expedition's horses.

Initially the prospects looked good for securing adequate food to sustain the party until the resumption of the journey. On May 14 Collins killed two bears, and Francois Labiche another with two cubs. The captains dispatched hunting parties in several directions to secure supplies for the dreaded crossing of the mountains. Sacagawea added to the diet by digging yampa, a fennel-like plant whose roots tasted like anise. Lewis considered yampa a "very agreeable food," which he believed helped to dispel the buildup of intestinal gas produced by the consumption of camas and cous. When some of the men complained of headaches and colic, the captains ascribed their debilities to the consumption of roots and bulbs, or possibly to the changes in weather.

Camp Choppunish proved a good situation. On the ridges above were conditions of late winter, where snow fell (in contrast to the rain along the river). On the high prairies but a day's travel to the east prevailed the fastness of winter. "Here we have

"We have come to a resolution to remove from hence to the quawmash grounds beyond Collins's creek on the 10th to hunt in that neighbourhood a few days, if possible lay in a stock of meat and then attempt the mountains about the middle of this month." Meriwether Lewis, June 3, 1806

Left: Basalt flow along Yakus Creek, west end of the Lolo Trail, near Weippe, Idaho

123

Summer, Spring and Winter within the Short Space of twenty or thirty miles," wrote Clark. "I am pleased at finding the river rise so rapidly," wrote Lewis on May 17, a condition he attributed to melting snow—"that icy barier which seperates me from my friends and Country, from all which makes life esteemable.—patience, patience." So the camp on the Clearwater was a time of watchful waiting.

Day after day, hunting parties fanned out to seek bear, deer, and trading opportunities. The lean times of Fort Clatsop repeated themselves on the Clearwater River. Occasionally the hunters had success and brought in a kill, or bartered successfully for camas and cous bread. The captains finally decided to allocate what remained of the slender inventory of trade goods and let each man barter for whatever supplies he could obtain. The individual trading kits were meager—an awl, a knitting pin, two needles, a yard of ribbon, half an ounce of vermilion, and a few skeins of thread—yet anxiety was low. "We eat the last morsel of meat which we had for dinner this evening," wrote Lewis on May 21, "yet nobody seems much conserned about the state of provision." Perhaps the men had lived too long at the edge; they seemed resigned to making do and, in this regard, accepted stoically their lot at the foot of the great mountains.

Ingenuity rose almost daily. When Lewis confronted a soaked chronometer, he disassembled the instrument, dried it with a feather, and treated its rusted parts with bear's oil, praying that it was none the worse for wear in spite of its rough treatment. When the trading stock seemed exhausted, the captains cut the brass buttons from their uniform coats, found two small metal boxes that had contained phosphorus, and added two empty phials to the bartering material. One of the men disengaged a small chain attached to a trap and transformed its links into needles or awls. These efforts squeezed the last possible potentials out of their goods and helped the party to build up a sufficient supply of food for the mountains.

Health became an important theme in the journals at Camp Choppunish. Poor health was a guarantee of getting noticed in the journals, just as someone's acting foolishly or failing to live up to the captains' expectations resulted in the recording of names and events in their daily notes. Jean Baptiste Charbonneau, son of Toussaint Charbonneau and Sacagawea, suffered ill health for several days and gained as much notice as he had at birth at Fort Mandan. Whether his ailment consisted of the complications of teething, tonsilitis, a mastoid infection, or mumps was unclear, but his treatments were intended to alleviate his fever and restless condition. The captains administered cream of tartar, flour of sulphur, and days of warm onion poultices to infected lymph nodes in his neck. Both Lewis and Clark were solicitous of the little boy and his care.

William Bratton, nearly unable to walk because of back pains and a probable herniated disc, was treated by John Shields with a time-tested strategy. Shields dug a pit in the earth, laid an intense fire, removed the coals, and seated Bratton on a board in the pit where he surrounded him with willow poles covered with blankets. While drinking large quantities of mint tea, Bratton dumped water into the pit and steamed himself as long as he could endure. The men then plunged Bratton twice into cold water, carried him back to the pit, steamed him another round, then let him cool slowly wrapped in blankets. Within a day he was walking. This curative also steadily improved the condition of a Nez Perce chief afflicted for three years with paralysis. The medical practices at Camp Choppunish brought results: Jean Baptiste Charbonneau recovered, Bratton resumed walking, and the Nez Perce chief was much improved.

The distribution of merchandise to the party inspired Shannon, Collins, and John Potts to take a newly made canoe across the Clearwater to trade for food. The current caught them broadside, swept the canoe into some trees, spilled the occupants, and sank the craft. Potts, a poor swimmer, barely escaped. The hapless men lost their merchandise, as well as three blankets and a valued blanket-coat. The river held down the canoe which, even when located by a party of Nez Perce men several days later,

"A plant growing in wet places with a single Stem, & leaves clasping round one another, no flowers observed. On the Kooskooskee, June 25th 1806."
Meriwether Lewis
Above: California false hellebore, Herbarium Sheet, (Veratrum californicum)

Right: Columnar basalt, a formation near Lewiston, Idaho

refused to dislodge from where it was pinned by flooding current. Baptiste Lepage and Charbonneau set out up the Clearwater to try to barter their items with the Nez Perce. Their horse fell off a steep cliff, came out on the opposite side, was sent back to them by the friendly Indians, but lost its inventory of goods. When the Indians tried to ferry over roots and other foodstuffs on a raft, it disintegrated, and they, too, lost everything for their efforts. The Clearwater, a river of life flowing through Nez Perce country, took much and yet—in spite of ardent hopes—produced no salmon.

Sergeant Ordway and his detachment returned to Camp Choppunish on June 2. A projected short trip over the ridges to buy salmon at the Nez Perce's fishery on the Salmon River had become an ordeal. The men covered nearly seventy miles in each direction. Although they brought back seventeen spring salmon, Lewis noted "the distance was so great from which they brought the fish that most of them were nearly spoiled."

Camp Choppunish provided time for the captains to catch up with their scientific observations. On May 31, Clark completed a map showing the country between the Missouri and Snake Rivers. In addition to stream courses, names, and other data, Clark recorded descriptive notes about distances and days of travel between key locations. The captains also recorded a weather log for May and entered a tally of the rising and falling of the Clearwater by the inches of change observed daily. To the daily log they appended "Remarks," some of them confirming the tantalizing frustration that gripped the party. On May 17, for example, they wrote: "the indians caught 3 salmon at their village on the Kooskooskee above our camp some miles. they say they cannot be caught as yet because those which first ascend the river do not keep near shore." The bountiful salmon were always close, but consistently beyond easy reach.

The days at Camp Choppunish yielded observations and specimens new to science. The ragged robin, a stunning wildflower (subsequently named *Clarkia pulchella* by Frederick Pursh in 1814), was among the discoveries. "Capt. L—s met with a *singular plant* in blume of which we preserved a Specimene," wrote Clark. Lewis's description was a model of technical precision. "This has the appearance of a monopetallous flower growing from the Center of the four petalled corollar which is rendered more conspicuous in consequence of the first being white and the latter of a pale purple," he wrote. "I regret very much that the Seed of this plant are not ripe as yet and it is probable will not be so dureing our residence in this neighbourhood."

Lewis described rattlesnakes, lizards, frogs, toads, horseflies, butterflies, tumble bugs, bumblebees, and caterpillars (which he termed the "Silk worm"). He tried to sort out the variegated hues of grizzly bears and whether or not they were of a single species. He discussed the appearance and habits of the Columbian ground squirrel and Lewis's woodpecker. Although sighted previously, the woodpecker had eluded capture, but on the Clearwater the party killed several. Lewis observed: "the belly and breast is of a curious mixture of white and blood red which has much the appearance of having been artificially painted or Stained of that colour, the red reather predominates." He examined head, eye, breast, feet, toes, nails, flying actions, feathering, and even the foods of this creature.

By the first week of June the Clearwater began dropping. The captains convinced themselves that the snow had melted. The Nez Perce counseled otherwise. On June 6 Clark and several men visited Chief Broken Arm, but learned that most of his people intended to wait until later in the summer to cross the mountains and that no young men had, as yet, been selected to accompany the Corps of Discovery. Clark thus concluded it was unlikely that he could hire guides from the Nez Perce. Some of the men who were with him bartered "little notions," the last of their goods, for roots and Indian bread.

The men began fixing their saddles, arranging provisions, and trading horses, such as the Nez Perce were willing to accept. The captains encouraged physical activity and remarked that those who had not been out hunting had become "reather lazy and

Left: Clearwater River, Idaho

"I met with a singular plant today in blume of which I preserved a specemine; it grows on the steep sides of the fertile hills near this place . . . . the corolla superior consists of four pale perple petals which are tripartite, the central lobe largest and all terminate obtusely . . . ." Meriwether Lewis, June 1, 1806

Above: Clarkia pulchella, named after William Clark

127

slouthfull." The men of the expedition thus engaged in hours of competition with the Nez Perce. George Drouillard and Reuben Fields emerged as champion foot racers. The men played the game of "prisoner's base" (a boys' game in which each side tries to make prisoners of the opposite side who run out of their base area), and in the evening listened to the violin and danced. Even the intelligence that the snow yet lay deep on the mountains, as disagreeable as it was, did not slow the pace. "Our party seem much elated with the idea of moving on towards their friends and country, they all seem allirt in their movements today," wrote Lewis on June 9. "They have every thing in readiness for a move."

Eagerness and wishful thinking led to the decision to set out on June 10. The expedition members broke up Camp Choppunish, left the Clearwater, and began the steep ascent of the slopes to the prairies at the base of the Bitterroots. Clark expressed confidence: "we Set out with the party each man being well mounted and a light load on a 2d horse, besides which we have several supernumary horses in case of accident or the want of provisions." In this moment of reflection, he concluded: "we therefore feel ourselves perfectly equiped for the Mountains."

Weippe Prairie was in the bloom of spring with redroot and ceanothus, wild rose, and camas. Lewis described the methods of the Nez Perce in cooking and preserving camas bulbs and wrote enthusiastically about this spring lily. Ducks and cranes frequented the swampy ground. The men, determined to save their food for the mountains, hunted squirrels for dinner. Hunters brought in eight deer and reported having wounded others and a bear. Food figured prominently in the journals, for the party knew and feared the conditions ahead.

With a bit of trepidation, the Corps of Discovery packed up and on June 14 set out into the forests of the watersheds of Collins and El Dorado Creeks. "Even now I Shudder with the expectation with great dificuelties in passing those Mountains," wrote Clark, "from the debth of Snow and the want of grass Sufficient to Subsist our horses." The fears were fully realized. Rain fell and the trail became a slippery, dangerous trace through dense woods strewn with downed timber. The men pressed on, fighting their way through wet underbrush and confusing terrain until, on June 16, they camped in a glade on El Dorado Creek, the last possible place to feed the horses before entering the higher elevation of the Bitterroots. The hold of winter was evident, for the brilliant yellow erythronium—avalanche lily—was just coming into bloom. At night the temperature plummeted toward freezing.

The following day—June 17—the immensity of the obstacles awaiting them overwhelmed the party. The men found Hungry Creek deep, rapid, and dangerous with snowmelt. On the ridges, the snow lay a dozen or more feet deep. The cold air benumbed hands and feet. Drouillard, the experienced hunter and scout, expressed doubts that it would be possible to find the way, especially when the journey would require a minimum of five days to press through to the upper Lochsa. "If we proceeded and should get bewildered in these mountains," reflected Lewis, "the certainty was that we should loose all our horses and consequently our baggage instruments perhaps our papers and thus eminently wrisk the loss of the discoveries which we had already made if we should be so fortunate as to escape with life." The captains had no choice—they had to turn back.

For the first time in their long journey, the members of the Corps of Discovery were unable to proceed. The captains ordered the men to construct platforms in the trees where they deposited and covered their instruments, papers, and critical foodstuffs. They concluded that the items would be safer cached deep in the forest than risked in the perilous terrain during a return to Weippe Prairie. "We began our retragrade march at 1 P.M.," wrote Clark, "haveing remain'd about three hours on this Snowey mountain." Drouillard and Shannon moved out all the way to the Clearwater River to try to find a guide. They carried a rifle as the inducement to any of the Nez Perce who would take the party through to the Bitterroot Valley.

Above: Pronghorn or antelope (Antilocapra americana)

"It rained moderately the greater part of the day and snowed as usual on the plain. Sergt. Pryor informed me that it was shoe deep this morning when he came down."
Meriwether Lewis,
May 16, 1806

Right: Idaho's Bitterroot Mountains

The perils of the route rose on all sides. During the difficult return to the prairie, John Potts slashed his leg with a large knife, and Lewis experienced considerable difficulty in stanching the flow of blood. John Colter's horse fell into Hungry Creek and was swept down the torrent some distance through sharp rocks and chilling water. Repeated efforts to gig fish yielded little return for the effort. When the men speared a few fish, they found that they were trout, not the spring salmon. Mosquitoes attacked with a vengeance. Many in the party were out of sorts. Lewis, for example, roasted morels that Pierre Cruzatte had gathered in the forest. "In this way," wrote Lewis, "I had for the first time the true taist of the morell which is truly an insippid taistless food." Stalked by hunger and troubled by their circumstances in the woods, the party concluded to return to Weippe Prairie and await word about a guide.

The narrow window of opportunity for crossing the Bitterroots plagued the thoughts of the captains. If Shannon and Drouillard failed to hire a guide, Lewis and Clark realized that they would have to try to find their way alone. They talked over the options. One of them would take four able woodsmen, three or four strong horses, and a good amount of supplies and proceed ahead, perhaps two days in advance of the main party. This patrol would seek the route by trying to locate where the horses and possessions of the Nez Perce had rubbed against the trees. They would blaze this route. Two men would return to guide the main party; the other two and one of the captains would press on to blaze more trail. If this failed, the entire expedition would return and move south, probably via the Snake River, and seek another route over the mountains to the homeland of the Shoshones via the Yellowstone country. That route, of course, was entirely unknown and perilous, for it would take them into the homeland of the Snake Indians, ardent foes of the Nez Perce.

Nearly a week passed while the men hunted, fished, traded, and waited. Drouillard and Shannon had taken several days to find willing guides, but when they returned on June 23, they had recruited three Nez Perce. For the price of two guns, the guides had agreed to accompany the expedition as far as the Great Falls. "These are all young men of good character and much respected by their nation," wrote Lewis. The following morning, horses collected, the party set out again. That evening, camped deep in the forest, the Nez Perce engaged in what the captains interpreted as an act to gain good conditions for travel. Lewis wrote:

> last evening the indians entertained us with seting the fir trees on fire. they have a great number of dry lims near their bodies which when set on fire creates a very suddon and immence blaze from bottom to top of those tall trees. they are a beatifull object in this situation at night. this exhibition reminded me of a display of fireworks.

The party found the cached instruments, papers, and specimens on the ridge, stopped to pack and to cook a meal of boiled venison and cous roots, and found that the snow had decreased nearly four feet. In some places, however, it yet lay seven feet deep on the trail. "Accordingly we set out with our guides who lead us over and along the steep sides of tremendious mountains entirely covered with snow," wrote Lewis. The party pressed on a considerable distance to find a camp used the previous September, where they found good grass for their horses. The Nez Perce knew the way; on June 27, at their request, the expedition halted at an elevated promontory where the guides wanted to smoke. "On this eminence," observed Lewis, "the natives have raised a conic mound of stones 6 or eight feet high and on it's summit erected a pine pole of 15 feet long." The noteworthy place provided a panoramic vista of the vast Bitterroot Range and produced this sobering reflection in the captains' journals: "without the assistance of our guides, I doubt much whether we who had passed them could find our way to Travellers rest in their present Situation for the marked trees on which we had placed Considerable reliance are much fewer and more difficult to find than we had apprehended."

"Their women brade their hair in two tresses which hang in the same position of those of the men. they also wear a cap or cup on the head formed of beargrass and cedar bark. the men also frequently attach some small ornament to a small plat of hair on the center of the crown of their heads."
Meriwether Lewis,
May 13, 1806
*Left: Bear grass
(Xerophyllum tenax)*

" . . . the first put forth from forty to fifty alternate pinate leaves which are sessile, horizontal, multipartite for half their length from the point of insertion and terminating in a long shaped apex . . . ."
Meriwether Lewis,
January 22, 1806
*Above: Bracken fern
(Pteridium acquilinum)*

"Between the great falls of the Columbia and this place, we saw more horses, than I ever before saw in the same space of country. They are not of the largest size of horses, but very good and active."
Patrick Gass, May 9, 1806
Above: Appaloosa horses

"Found the river very high indeed. Swam the horses across and got across in an Indian canoe as our men informed us that as Some of our men were crossing several days past our large canoe ran against Some trees as they were going to Shore and the canoe upset and Sank emediately."
John Ordway, June 2, 1806
Right: Lochsa River, Idaho

Conditions remained mixed in the party. John Potts's leg was swollen, but appeared to respond to treatment with herbal poultices. Clark suffered from headaches. Camping in a meadow of bear grass on the steep mountainside, the captains issued a pint of bear's oil to each mess group. The men consumed the oil with boiled roots. On June 28 they passed the place where they had ascended from Wendover Ridge on the upper Lochsa the previous year. The travel route was across deep snow that, though slippery, covered rocks and the jackstraws of downed timber. Finally on June 29 they arrived at Packer Meadows—the top of Lolo Pass. That evening they camped at Lolo Hot Springs and soaked the chills of the Bitterroots out of their bodies. "Both the men and Indians amused themselves with the use of a bath this evening," wrote Lewis. "In this bath which had been prepared by the Indians by stoping the run with stone and gravel, I bathed and remained in 19 minutes, it was with dificulty I could remain thus long and it caused a profuse sweat," he concluded.

Thus, for a second time, the Corps of Discovery had traversed the mighty Bitterroots, the greatest physical and mental challenge of their entire journey. The tally of trials was great: vexing weeks of waiting, uncertainty about the route, exposure to cold, near starvation, slippery trails, and accidents. Though emotions ran a bit raw, the finely tuned crew endured, and survived. Ahead lay Traveler's Rest, their old camp in the Bitterroot Valley. And beyond that, the splitting up of the command for special reconnaissance missions during the return trip into the watershed of the Missouri. The quest for the Pacific was in hand. From this point on, the party was on its way home.

"After dinner we proceeded up the creek about 1/2 a mile, passing it three times, thence through a high broken country to an Easterly fork of the same creek about 10 1/2 miles and incamped near a small prairie in the bottom land."
Meriwether Lewis, June 15, 1806

"So we halted on the top of this mountain and our officers consulted on what was best to do. at length determined to our Sorrow to return to where we might git feed for our horses."
John Ordway, June 17, 1806

Left: Clouds above the Lochsa River, near Smoking Place in the Bitteroot Mountains, Idaho

Above: Small prairie camp, June 15, 1806, Eldorado Creek, Idaho

"Took the mountains and the road So bad Several of our horses fell   about noon we had Thunder and hard Showers of rain. we crossed Several runs on which is considerable white ceedar timber balsom fer & diffrent kinds of pine . . . ." John Ordway, June 15, 1806
Overleaf: Western red cedars (Thuja plicata) *at Bernard DeVoto Grove, Crooked Creek, Idaho*

Epilogue

The transit of the Pacific Northwest consumed more than eleven months, from July 1805 to June 1806. During that time, the Corps of Discovery passed through an unknown land, dealing daily with unfamiliar tribes and coping with unexpected weather conditions. Previous explorations had only nibbled at the edges of the region by charting the coast and examining the Columbia estuary. Lewis and Clark plumbed the region's depths and did so by summoning leadership, ingenuity, fortitude, and trust. The members of the expedition accomplished all of this, and at the same time furthered the diplomatic, scientific, and commercial goals laid down by President Jefferson. Their labors in the vast region west of the Louisiana Purchase catapulted the expedition to international significance. And the party's explorations dramatically enhanced the United States' "discovery rights" to what became known as the Oregon Country (Idaho, Oregon, Washington, Western Montana).

Penetration of the Pacific Northwest by the Corps of Discovery ended any hope of a water route for commerce across the continent, but it made clear the tremendous potential of the western part of North America. Lewis and Clark reported on the abundance of fur-bearing animals and fish runs; the moderate climate, fertile soils, and peaceful Native peoples; and the far-flung river system of the Columbia. Their journey into the great unknown set in motion forces that culminated in 1846, when the United States secured claim to all the lands between the forty-second and forty-ninth parallels. Acquisition of the region beyond the Rockies, first explored by the Lewis and Clark Expedition, completed America's quest to become a continental nation.

The Corps of the Discovery traveled east from the Bitterroot Valley and arrived in St. Louis the last week of September 1806. The adventures beyond the mountains were many, but the focus was on getting home. The journey west had been a unified pursuit, but once the expedition reached the Bitterroot Valley, the captains split up their command. Lewis departed with a small detachment via the Clark Fork to the northern plains, his mission to determine whether the Marias River took its headwaters north of the forty-ninth parallel. Clark took the remainder of the party to Camp Fortunate on the Beaverhead and on to Three Forks, where he split the men. Some he sent down the Missouri to the Great Falls to await the arrival of Lewis from his northern reconnaissance; with the remainder of the expedition, Clark explored the Yellowstone to its confluence with the Missouri.

The grand design worked. Somehow, in spite of the remote country through which they traveled, the commanders and men displayed unerring skills in synchronization and, by appointment, met a short distance below the mouth of the Yellowstone. Clark wrote on August 12: "at meridian Capt Lewis hove in Sight with the party which went by way of the Missouri as well as that which accompanied him from Travellers rest on Clarks river." Concern was high, for Pierre Cruzatte had three days before accidentally shot Lewis in the buttocks, mistaking him for an elk. Lewis, in great discomfort, lay face down in a pirogue with lint stuffed in the draining bullet hole. Clark noted: "I examined the wound and found it a very bad flesh wound the ball had passed through the fleshy part of his left thy below the hip bone and cut the cheek of the right buttock for 3 inches in length and the debth of the ball."

The wounding of Captain Lewis was not the only story the group had to tell. During the reconnaissance of the Marias, Lewis and his small detachment had become involved in hostilities. Perhaps at no other point in the expedition was so much at stake as when the vulnerable squad under Lewis's command fell into conflict with the Blackfeet. He and only six men had entered a region where it was widely known that trespassers were not welcome. His explorations confirmed that the Marias watershed lay south of the forty-ninth parallel—then a dispute erupted when some Blackfeet young men seized the firearms of the patrol. "Damn you! Let go my gun!" resounded through the early morning quiet. The words of George Drouillard were prelude to a scuffle, then armed conflict. The young Blackfeet scrambled for firearms and tried to

"Had a Shower of hail and Thunder. about 1 oClock P.M. we arived at the glades of the rockey mountn. Crossed glade Creek Several times and halted at a handsom flat of grass and Commass." John Ordway, June 29, 1806

Left: Camas at Packer Meadows/Glade Creek, Lolo Pass, Idaho-Montana

Above: Camas (Camassia quamash), a primary food for native peoples

run off the patrol's horses. Lewis and his men recovered their arms and horses and fled. They left a Blackfeet man dead, a peace medal ominously hanging around his neck, and another gravely wounded. The reconnaissance of the Marias concluded in a wild dash of one hundred miles to the Missouri River and escape from the northern plains.

Below the mouth of the Yellowstone, evidence of changing times greeted the men. Flowing up the Missouri was a flood of commerce. The Rocky Mountain fur trade was underway. John Colter, in fact, decided not to return to "civilization" in St. Louis; he hired on with a party headed to the distant mountains. Colter was more at home in the wilds than in American society. The nation was in a ferment of growth and grappling with disputes with Great Britain. It was headed, inevitably, toward the War of 1812.

In many ways the Lewis and Clark Expedition met and exceeded President Jefferson's instructions. The captains had not found a practicable water route for commerce between the United States and Asia by way of the interior of the continent, but they had achieved much more. The expedition fired American imaginations about the prospect of expansion from sea to sea and drove the agenda of crafting a continental nation.

In science, diplomacy, and general knowledge, the explorers achieved much. They produced more than one hundred manuscript maps of the lands through which they traveled. They dispelled the mythic geography of a single mountain range in the West and filled in astounding detail about the watersheds of the Missouri and Columbia Rivers. They opened diplomatic relations with Indian tribes, initiated trade dealings, and introduced Native Americans to new technologies and cultures. They collected word lists, ethnographic data, botanical and zoological specimens, and recorded hundreds of thousands of words of candid observations about the American West.

The journals of the expedition—from that of Patrick Gass published in 1807, to the two-volume, abridged diaries of Lewis and Clark edited in 1814 by Nicholas Biddle and Paul Allen—fed a public hungry for information about the far reaches of North America. One measure of that interest is the appearance of numerous apocryphal books about the expedition (published, for example, in Philadelphia, 1809; London, 1809; Lebanon, Pennsylvania, 1811; Frederick, Maryland, 1812; Baltimore, 1812; Philadelphia, 1812; and Baltimore, 1813). The Gass journal had multiple printings (Pittsburgh, 1807; London, 1808; Paris, 1810; Philadelphia, 1810, 1811, 1812; and Weimar, 1814). Once the Biddle-Allen edition of Lewis and Clark's accounts appeared in 1814, it too drew wide interest with editions in London (1814, 1815, 1817); Dublin (1817); Te Dordrecht, Netherlands (1816); and a further abridged version in Vienna (1826).

The Pacific quest of Lewis and Clark fulfilled the leap of imagination of the philosopher-president, Thomas Jefferson. As a leader, Jefferson embraced the life of the mind; he was both politician and scholar, a practical man and a man of science. In sending Lewis and Clark to the Pacific Ocean, he unleashed events of incalculable consequence. In their travels from Three Forks to the Pacific and back to the Missouri watershed, Lewis and Clark passed through a land unknown to a wider world. They unlocked the mysteries of the interior of a vast continent. Their quest for the source of the Missouri and the cognate headwaters of the tributaries of the Columbia was akin to subsequent explorations seeking the source of the Nile—but Lewis and Clark's mission helped chart the destiny of a nation, whereas trips to exotic places in other lands became the source of grand adventure narratives.

The journals, maps, and natural history collections of Lewis and Clark confirmed that significant parts of western North America were fertile, inhabited, productive, and filled with promise. The fur trade beckoned alluringly, as did the fertile soils of the Columbia Plateau and Willamette Valley. The towering forests, vast runs of fish, and promise of minerals suggested unparalleled opportunities. The successful quest of these explorers to penetrate the unknown interior of the Pacific Northwest helped set the growing nation on its course.

"There are two speceis of the wild rose both quinqui petallous and of a damask red but the one is as large as the common red rose of our gardens."
Meriwether Lewis,
June 10, 1806
Right: Nootka rose (Rosa nutkana), Chief Timothy Reserve, Idaho

Acknowledgments

This volume emerged through the chemistry of connections—with the land, Lewis & Clark enthusiasts, teaching successive generations of students at Lewis & Clark College, and compelling friendships. To Robert Reynolds, photographer and collaborator in this and other adventures in history, I owe much; and likewise to his cheerful design associate, Letha Wulf, I extend my appreciation. Both seek the positives in life and draw the best out of others. Clay Straus Jenkinson has inspired me with new insights into the literature of the Lewis and Clark Expedition. He has walked my legs off in the Bitterroots, tested my assumptions, entertained me with thousands of lines of memorized poetry, and probed my sense of history. America's model humanist, he has role-played Thomas Jefferson and Meriwether Lewis to such a degree that, I confess, I have trouble separating these historical figures from their humanist interpreter!

My late friends—Dr. Eldon G. Chuinard, Robert Lange, and Irving Anderson—persuaded me that I must teach Lewis and Clark Expedition history. The gracious gifts of the Chuinard and Anderson libraries to Lewis & Clark College have helped make that possible. To Roger Wendlick, who read and commented on my drafts in light of his years of collecting Lewis & Clarkiana, I am most appreciative. A better manuscript the consequence of several hands and more than one head. I also extend my appreciation to Douglas Erickson and Jeremy Skinner of the College Archives and Heritage Room, Watzek Library, Lewis & Clark College.

There are also those with whom I have stepped into the history of the Lewis and Clark Expedition in the Pacific Northwest. These include dozens of former students who braved the Lolo Trail and Clearwater River in summer expeditions; Mike Hopkins, Doug Pfeiffer, and Rob Reynolds, who paddled the Columbia estuary with me in sea kayaks; four U.S. Forest Service "intensive semesters" traveling from the Bitterroots to Portland in the "footsteps of Lewis and Clark"; two Stanford seminars following the expedition's water route from the Clearwater to the Pacific; two Lewis & Clark College expeditions to the Lolo Trail and points west; and one National Geographic Society seminar to the upper Missouri country. To all who endured, read, questioned, and probed the professor during these field-based educational experiences—thank you.

Robert Reynolds and I also extend our appreciation to the Maryhill Museum, Missouri Historical Society, National Park Service (Fort Clatsop, Nez Perce National Historical Park, and Independence Park), Oregon Historical Society, Beinecke Library of Yale University, Portland District—Army Corps of Engineers, and Watzek Library of Lewis & Clark College for historical images used in this volume. We particularly thank Ron Ackerman for assistance in securing the photo of wapato and Linda Paisano for help at Spalding, Idaho. Additionally, we would like to thank Ted Gibbs, Francine Havercroft, Joline Hope, Tom Metz, and Colleen Schafroth.

To my wife, Patti, and my children—Andrew Dow and Ann-Marie—for enduring my many absences, I am also appreciative. These forays into history charge the batteries and make life both exciting and rewarding.

Bibliography

Works consulted for writing these essays included both primary and secondary sources. All quotations are drawn from *The Journals of the Lewis & Clark Expedition* (Moulton 1983-99). Quoted words open with an initial capital letter when such modern usage is appropriate. All other material is quoted as spelled and punctuated in the Moulton edition.

Ambrose, Stephen E. *Undaunted Courage: Meriwether Lewis, Thomas Jefferson, and the Opening of the American West.* New York: Simon & Schuster, 1996.

Cutright, Paul Russell. *A History of the Lewis and Clark Journals.* Norman, OK: University of Oklahoma Press, 1976.

———. *Lewis and Clark: Pioneering Naturalists.* Urbana, IL: University of Illinois Press, 1969; reprint, Lincoln, NE: University of Nebraska Press, 1989.

Furtwangler, Albert. *Acts of Discovery: Visions of America in the Lewis and Clark Journals.* Urbana, IL: University of Illinois Press, 1993.

Jackson, Donald, ed. *Letters of the Lewis and Clark Expedition with Related Documents, 1783-1854.* 2nd ed., 2 vols. Urbana, IL: University of Illinois Press, 1978.

———. *Thomas Jefferson & the Stony Mountains: Exploring the West from Monticello.* Urbana, IL: University of Illinois Press, 1981.

Jenkinson, Clay Straus. *The Character of Meriwether Lewis: 'Completely Metamorphosed' in the American West.* Reno, NV: The Marmarth Institute, 2000.

Moulton, Gary, ed. *The Journals of the Lewis & Clark Expedition.* 12 vols. Lincoln, NE: University of Nebraska Press, 1983-99.

Ronda, James P. *Finding the West: Explorations with Lewis and Clark.* Albuquerque, NM: University of New Mexico Press, 2001.

———. *Lewis and Clark Among the Indians.* Lincoln, NE: University of Nebraska Press, 1984.

Ronda, James P., ed. *Voyages of Discovery: Essays on the Lewis and Clark Expedition.* Helena, MT: Montana Historical Society Press, 1998.

Space, Ralph S. *The Lolo Trail: A History of Events Connected With the Lolo Trail since Lewis and Clark.* Lewiston, ID: Printcraft Printing, 1970.

Strong, Emory and Ruth. *Seeking Western Waters: The Lewis and Clark Trail from the Rockies to the Pacific.* Herbert K. Beals, ed. Portland, OR: Oregon Historical Society Press, 1995.

Suttles, Wayne, ed. *Handbook of North American Indians, Vol. 7, Northwest Coast.* Washington, D.C.: Smithsonian Institution, 1990.

Walker, Deward, ed. *Handbook of North American Indians, Vol. 12, Plateau.* Washington, D.C.: Smithsonian Institution, 1998.